Critical Guides to Spanish Texts

27 Garcilaso de la Vega: Poems

Critical Guides to Spanish Texts

EDITED BY J. E. VAREY AND A. D. DEYERMOND

GARCILASO DE LA VEGA

Poems

A Critical Guide

Elias L. Rivers
Professor of Spanish
State University of New York
at Stony Brook, Long Island

Grant & Cutler Ltd *in association with*
Tamesis Books Ltd 1980

I.S.B.N. 84-499-4506-2

DEPÓSITO LEGAL: v. 740 - 1981

Printed in Spain by
Artes Gráficas Soler, S. A. - Olivereta, 28 - Valencia (18)
for
GRANT AND CUTLER LTD
11 BUCKINGHAM STREET, LONDON, W.C.2.

Dedicated to my students

whose questions and answers
have contributed to this book.

Contents

Preface

REFERENCES to the text of Garcilaso's poetry are based upon my own edition of his *Poesías castellanas completas,* volume 6 in the Clásicos Castalia series. The other economical edition, kept in print since 1911, is that of T. Navarro Tomás, volume 3 in the Clásicos Castellanos series. These two texts are substantially the same; so are the titles and line numbers, except for the *coplas* and Sonnets XXX-XL. For more scholarly annotations, see the more expensive editions of A. Gallego Morell (Madrid: Gredos, 1972) and of E. L. Rivers (Madrid: Castalia, 1974).

The figures in parentheses in italic type refer to the numbered items in the Bibliographical Note; where necessary these are followed by page numbers. (For comprehensive bibliographies see the more expensive editions mentioned above.) My biographical sketch of Garcilaso is based primarily upon Hayward Keniston's critical study, supplemented by the articles of San Román, Goodwyn, García Rey and Martínez Ferrando.

I am grateful to the editors of this series, Professor A. D. Deyermond and Professor J. E. Varey, for a number of helpful suggestions.

E. L. R.

Stony Brook, Long Island
January, 1980

1. Critical and Biographical Introduction

MODERN Spanish poetry begins with Garcilaso. Poetry written before him sounds distinctly medieval to the twentieth-century reader. But his poetry, though written over four hundred years ago, is still read as modern poetry, and still influences contemporary poets in a direct way. To cite only one example, *La voz a ti debida* (1934) by Pedro Salinas is a sequence of love poems such as Garcilaso might have written in witty sonnets; the title itself is taken from Garcilaso's Third Eclogue. For this reason the present study is an attempt to present Garcilaso's poetry, not as an archaeological curiosity, but primarily as living literature. Garcilaso's Latin and Italian sources have been noted by scholars ever since the sixteenth century. But such an emphasis would have been out of place here, for it would involve a detailed examination of texts in three foreign languages.

What most modern readers need is a guide to the understanding of each poem written by Garcilaso. It is misleading to think that Garcilaso had one characteristic style, or personal attitude toward life, to be found everywhere in his poetry. The concept of a homogeneous personal style is not valid even for many post-Romantic poets. For a classical poet like Garcilaso, the search for different attitudes, defined in part by traditional genres, must be the primary approach, or process of orientation. Once the basic attitudes, or genres, have been defined, the reader can then focus clearly upon those more personal stylistic details which give vital texture to the poetry as a whole.

Garcilaso, Spain's first great Renaissance poet, is one of the few Spanish authors to have freed himself from the provincial traditionalism of his native land to become a cos-

mopolitan resident of Italy. He was born in Toledo, probably
in 1501, the second son of an aristocratic family of some
literary distinction. His father had been for a time the ambas-
sador of Ferdinand and Isabella in Rome. The boy himself
was raised in Toledo, where he studied Latin in the new
humanistic mode established in Spain by Antonio de Nebrija.
He undoubtedly learned much of Virgil and Ovid by heart,
as was the custom in such schools. He was also initiated into
the courtly arts of music (he played the lute and the harp),
fencing, equitation and hunting. His father died when Garcilaso was about eleven years old, and with his older brother
away at Court, the boy grew up under the affectionate influence
of his mother, Doña Sancha de Guzmán, who had an estate of
her own, the castle and little town of Batres, between Toledo
and Madrid.

Toledo, the ancient Visigothic capital of Spain, and a
clerical stronghold as the seat of the primate of the Spanish
Church, had more than its share of civil tensions. After the
expulsion of practicing Jews in 1492, a strong middle-class
community of converts and their descendants found itself under
a growing pressure of racial discrimination against "new
Christians" by the less wealthy populace and by the "old
Christian" farmers of the province. This convert community
tended to ally itself with the aristocracy, for which it had
long performed services in financial affairs and tax collect-
ing. Struggling to maintain traditional feudal rights, or *fueros,*
this alliance provided a conservative resistance to totalitarian
pressures from the populace and the monarchy. Another threat
to the municipal establishment in Toledo was that of the
cathedral chapter, which also held considerable financial and
administrative power. In 1519 Garcilaso was involved in a
local riot; he supported the town council against the cathedral
chapter in a conflict over control of a hospital. For this he
was exiled from the town for three months. Clearly he was,
if not anticlerical, at least an advocate of the local lay and
civil authorities.

Events of the following year indicate that Garcilaso still
had the confidence of the Toledan municipality. His older

brother, Don Pedro Laso de la Vega, because of his violent opposition to the new king, Charles of Hapsburg, had been sentenced to exile from Spain and could therefore not represent Toledo at the Cortes, or Parliament, assembled by Charles in Santiago de Compostela. Garcilaso was sent instead, as Procurador Mayor (municipal representative), to state Toledo's opposition to the king's demand for special new taxes to be levied upon municipalities. According to a contemporary account, Garcilaso told the king that:

> él traía un memorial estrución de su ciudad de las cosas que había de hacer y conferir en las Cortes, que las viese su alteza y de aquello no le mandase exceder, porque erraría, y que aquello haría y cumpliría en la mejor manera que su alteza fuese servido. En otra manera, que antes consintiría hacerse cuartos y su alteza mandarle cortar la cabeza antes de consentir ni otorgar cosa de tanto perjuicio de su ciudad y del reino. (*35*, p. 227)

But fortunately for Garcilaso's own development, and for the history of Spanish poetry, the nineteen-year-old youth was somehow converted to the royal cause. He was named a member of the Court and, when civil war broke out, he fought for the king against the Comunero rebellion, which in Toledo was led by his own older brother, Don Pedro. At the battle of Olías, near Toledo, on August 17, 1521, Garcilaso received his first wound. A year later in Palencia he rejoined the Court of the victorious king and newly elected Emperor, Charles V. From this point on, our poet's career was closely associated with the rapid rise of Spain as a dominant power in Europe. Turning his back upon the provincial culture of Toledo, he entered an international atmosphere of Erasmian reform and Renaissance humanism, in the service of a prince capable of using Spanish troops to sack Papal Rome.

At the Emperor's Court Garcilaso met the bilingual poet from Barcelona, Juan Boscán, and also Don Pedro de Toledo, of the Alva family. With them he joined in 1522 an unsuccessful expedition to rescue the knights of Rhodes, besieged by the Turks. Upon his return to the Spanish Court, on August

23, 1523, Garcilaso was elected to membership of the Military Order of Santiago (St James); with the Emperor's approval, he was knighted by his friend and patron Don Pedro de Toledo in Pamplona, where an army was being organized to cross the Pyrenees. After occupying Sauveterre, imperial troops early in 1524 took the frontier fortress of Fuenterrabía, near San Sebastián. During this campaign Garcilaso undoubtedly got to know the sixteen-year-old nephew of Don Pedro, Don Fernando de Toledo, soon to become the famous third Duke of Alva. To him he would devote almost half of his long Second Eclogue and all of his First Elegy.

After his noviciate of one year, in August of 1525, Garcilaso was given a noble bride by the Emperor. Doña Elena de Zúñiga and he signed matrimonial contracts which indicate clearly their considerable wealth in real estate, if not in cash. They established their home in Toledo, living at first in his mother's house. There is no indication that this aristocratic marriage was based upon romantic affection; it seems rather to have been a matter of social convenience. Doña Elena had been a lady-in-waiting of the Emperor's sister, Lady Eleanor of Austria. The latter's engagement to the captive king of France, Francis I, took place in Illescas, between Madrid and Toledo, in February of 1526, shortly after Garcilaso's own marriage.

In March of the same year the Emperor's Court went to Seville and Granada for six months to celebrate Charles V's marriage to Isabella of Portugal. Two of the distinguished Italian envoys to this wedding had a great deal to say of interest to Garcilaso's friend and fellow-poet Boscán. One was the Papal Nuncio Baldassare Castiglione, author of *Il Cortigiano (The Courtier);* when it was finally published two years later, Garcilaso was to encourage Boscán to translated it, brilliantly, into Spanish. The other was Andrea Navagero, an eminent humanist of Venice; in Granada he urged Boscán to try using in Spanish the eleven-syllable metrics of Italian poetry. Boscán tells us that his first experiments of this sort were done as he rode from Granada to Barcelona, and that Garcilaso soon began to collaborate with him on this project.

It is from 1526, then, that we can date the beginnings of the Renaissance revolution in Spanish poetry. Also in Granada was another person destined to have an impact upon Garcilaso and the poetry he was to write; this was Doña Isabel Freire, an attractive young lady in the retinue of the Portuguese princess Isabella. [1]

Between 1526 and 1529 Garcilaso led an externally quiet life. He divided his time between the Court, wherever it was located in Spain, and his family in Toledo, where in March of 1528 he bought a house of his own. By the end of that year he and his wife had three sons: Garcilaso de la Vega, Íñigo de Zúñiga and Pedro de Guzmán. He also had an illegitimate son named Lorenzo, mentioned in his will, drawn in 1529. And in the same document Garcilaso mentioned a certain country girl from Extremadura, named Elvira, for whose loss of virginity he considered himself probably responsible. But his great love, the one which informs his best lyric poetry, was apparently the Portuguese lady, Isabel Freire, who continued

---

[1] The accepted view, which I follow here, namely that Isabel Freire may be in some sense identified with the Galatea and Elisa of Garcilaso's eclogues and perhaps with anonymous ladies appearing in some of his sonnets and *canciones,* has recently been questioned by Frank Goodwyn (*36*). Certainly this matter involves problems, both practical and theoretical: no one's erotic life is adequately documented in archives of any sort, and the connection between historical experiences and poetic texts is never direct or simple. But it was a literary convention of the Renaissance for the poet to refer, in a veiled way, to a muse, or idealized lady, identifiable with someone belonging to his own historical world, however distant she may actually have been. This literary convention was especially prevalent in pastoral fictions: a shepherdess or nymph often represented a lady in disguise. Such semi-secret identifications were more accessible to contemporaries than they are to us. Hence, the best evidence in this case is the title of Garcilaso's Copla II, first published by Brocense in 1574 as "Canción, habiéndose casado su dama": in the most authoritative surviving sixteenth-century Garcilaso manuscript this same poem is identified as "De Garcilaso a doña Ysabel Freyra [sic] porque se casó con un hombre fuera de su condición". This identification is accepted by such scrupulous modern scholars as Rafael Lapesa; but Pamela Waley (*61*) is right to assert the primary significance of literary traditions, and not of biographical legends.

to accompany the queen at Court. We know nothing concrete
about their relationship. Even if she was kindly disposed
toward him, her honour and that of the Spanish Court were
at stake; they could perhaps only converse discreetly. It was
however a cruel blow to Garcilaso when she was finally
betrothed, between October 1528 and March 1529, while the
Court was in Toledo, to Don Antonio de Fonseca, Lord of
Toro, nicknamed "the Fat". It is with reference to this episode
that we can understand autobiographically the first half of
Garcilaso's best-known poem, the First Eclogue.

On March 9 1529 the Court left Toledo and headed
for Italy, where Charles V wanted to be crowned Emperor
by the Pope himself. After a month spent in Zaragoza, the
Court reached Barcelona toward the end of April. On July
25, two days before embarking, Garcilaso signed his last will
and testament. The first portion is written in a legal hand
with all the formulas necessary to establish an entailed estate
for Garcilaso's oldest son. His possessions in the regions of
Toledo and Badajoz are taken into account. Then, in his own
handwriting, Garcilaso wrote an appendix which is of considerable human interest. He began by setting aside certain sums
for Masses and for works of charity. In a manner reflecting
an Erasmian anti-ceremonialism, he made it clear that he did
not want his burial to be a social affair: "No conviden a nadie
para mis honras, ni haya sermón en ellas." For his illegitimate
son Lorenzo he prescribed a university education first in humanistic literature and then, if clerically inclined, in canon
law, and if not, in civil law. He noted that the king owed him
some 200 ducats in back pay. And finally he listed his own
debts, some dating from as far back as the French campaign
of 1523; it is clear that he considered it a matter both of
honor and of religious duty to pay off every debt, if not in
money, in Masses, as judged best by a well-informed cleric.
Some of these debts are trivial, such as the money he owed
his barber; others are formal loans made against jewelry and
silver belonging to his wife and to his mother. The debt of
honor due to Elvira, the country girl, was estimated at
something less than twenty-seven ducats. The first witnesses

to his signature were his friend Juan Boscán and his older brother Pedro Laso de la Vega.

Two days later the imperial fleet of some hundred vessels left Barcelona, arriving in Genoa on August 12, 1529. By the early part of November the Court was established in Bologna. Between then and April 1530 we can imagine Garcilaso's first intensive exposure to the language, literature and culture of Italy. In April he returned to Spain. After a brief visit with his family in Toledo, he was sent to the French Court to give the Spanish queen's best wishes to her sister-in-law, Eleanor of Austria, who had finally married Francis I. Garcilaso was instructed to take notes on frontier fortifications and on the political atmosphere of France. He left for France toward the end of August, and by April 1531 he was back in Toledo.

On August 14, 1531, Garcilaso witnessed the betrothal of his nephew, the son of Don Pedro, to the heiress of the Duchy of Alburquerque, Doña Isabel de la Cueva. The Emperor was opposed to this match because of Don Pedro's Comunero activities of ten years previous. As a consequence, Garcilaso was arrested at the Basque town of Tolosa in February 1532 while he was accompanying the young Duke of Alva on an expedition to the Emperor's Court in Germany. After considerable cross-examination, he was formally exiled; he thereupon continued across the Pyrenees with the duke. We can follow their journey in Garcilaso's Second Eclogue, ll. 1433-1504: from the frontier to Paris to Utrecht to Cologne to Regensburg (Ratisbon), where they finally caught up with the Emperor in late March. The Emperor immediately had Garcilaso confined to an island in the Danube, a confinement clearly referred to in his Canción III. Afterwards he was allowed to continue his exile in Naples, of which Pedro de Toledo was named viceroy in early July. Garcilaso may well have participated in the Emperor's campaign against the Turkish besiegers of Vienna (see Second Eclogue, ll. 1505-1691) before leaving for Naples, which he reached in any case no later than November 1532.

For the rest of his life Garcilaso resided principally in
Naples, and it was here that he reached full maturity as a
Renaissance courtier and as a major Spanish poet. Prior to
this period he had written little poetry of significance; four
canzoni and a few sonnets in a predominantly Petrarchan mode
could not compete with Boscán's full-scale *canzoniere* of ten
songs and almost a hundred sonnets of a similar character.
Only Garcilaso's Canción III, presumably written while he was
confined in 1532 to the island in the Danube, anticipates the
mature style of his eclogues. But in Naples, from 1533 to
1536, he was in close contact with several distinguished Italian
humanists and poets. He was associated with a local academy,
which concentrated on the composition of Latin verse; Antonio Minturno is no doubt the best-known member of this
group. The memory of Sannazaro, a member who had died in
1530, was still very much alive; his works, in Latin and in
Italian, were studied and imitated. Among vernacular poets
Garcilaso was particularly well acquainted with Luigi Tansillo,
Bernardo Tasso and Giulio Cesare Caracciolo. There were
also humanists from Spain: Juan de Valdés and Juan Ginés de
Sepúlveda. Bilingual communication was no problem within the
brilliant Hispano-Italian court of Don Pedro de Toledo. Garcilaso was soon well known for his social presence and his
poems in Latin and in Spanish. And he undoubtedly became
involved in flirtations and love affairs with the delightfully
light ladies of Naples; one of these is mentioned, anonymously,
in his Second Elegy.

Garcilaso was one of the Viceroy's chief lieutenants and
envoys. In April 1533, for example, he carried letters to the
Emperor in Barcelona. And while there he revised with Boscán
the latter's translation of Castiglione's *Cortigiano,* a copy of
which Garcilaso had sent to Barcelona some time before;
Boscán's brilliant version, a model of Renaissance Spanish
prose, was published toward the end of the year, with a
prologue by Garcilaso. After a brief visit with his family,
Garcilaso was back in Naples by June. To this period belongs,
apparently, the composition of the so-called Second Eclogue

(the first one of three written), Garcilaso's longest and most ambitious work.

During the following year Garcilaso made two similar trips to Spain, and it was probably on one of these that he learned of the death in childbirth of Doña Isabel Freire. It was on his way back to Naples for the second time in 1534, in Avignon on October 12, that he wrote his Epistle in blank verse to Boscán. His First Eclogue, a poetic résumé of his love for Isabel Freire, was probably written in Naples toward the end of this year. In October 1534 the Emperor appointed him chatelain of Reggio, in the kingdom of Naples. It would seem from this that Garcilaso was planning to settle permanently in Italy, even though such an appointment, a sign of Charles V's favor, must have marked the end of his formal sentence of exile.

But our poet was not to have more than a few months of peace. By the spring of 1535 we find him on another military expedition, this time in North Africa. Landing in June near the ancient ruins of Carthage, Spanish troops besieged the pirate Barbarossa's fortress of La Goleta. Here Garcilaso was wounded slightly, but joined the Emperor's triumphal entry into Tunis on July 22. A month later these troops were back in the Sicilian port of Trapani. There the Duke of Alva's younger brother, Don Bernardino de Toledo, died, and Garcilaso addressed to the duke his First Elegy, a message of sympathy and stoic exhortation. He also wrote, during this lull in Sicily, his Second Elegy, an epistle in tercets to Boscán in Barcelona, telling him of his jealous fears with regard to a love whom he had had to leave behind in Naples. In both of these elegies we find the poet tired of war and politics, yearning for a more peaceful life.

In November the Emperor's troops returned to Naples, where their African victory was celebrated for several months. Garcilaso, high in Charles V's favor once more, was complimented by the great Bembo for his Latin odes; we have one dating from this period and addressed to Juan Ginés de Sepúlveda, imperial historian and humanist. This was the culmination of Garcilaso's military and literary career, for in less than a year he would be dead, at the age of thirty-five.

In the spring of 1536 Garcilaso had to resign as chatelain of Reggio in order to engage in a new campaign with the Emperor. He was put in command of three thousand fresh troops from Spain, who disembarked near Savona in late May to fight against the French invaders of Italy. In mid-July we find him in Savigliano writing his last letter to a friend in Naples. It must have been about this time that he wrote his last great poem, the Third Eclogue, dedicated to the wife of his friend and patron the Viceroy of Naples.

The invasion of Provence went very badly. On September 19, 1536, Garcilaso was mortally wounded as he tried to lead his men in scaling the Tower of Muy, near Fréjus. He died in Nice on the 14th of October. Despite his instructions that he be buried wherever he died, his family brought the body back from southern France to the local convent Church of San Pedro Mártir in Toledo.

Garcilaso's life, then, can be seen as a process of movement away from the provincial particularism of Spanish life in Toledo toward the more international attitudes of Charles V's court and finally into the humanistic cosmopolitanism of Renaissance Italy. In Naples he discovered his essential spiritual kinship with Virgil and Sannazaro, from whose eclogues he did not feel separated as a poet by time or language. Of later Spanish authors only Cervantes could approach the European detachment, the Montaignean spirit, of this cosmopolitan aristocrat from Toledo.

The following chapters cover the three main groups of Garcilaso's poetry, as arranged generically in the first edition. His fragmentary Petrarchan *canzoniere,* in which medieval courtly love and classical landscapes and myths are juxtaposed, is seen to reflect Garcilaso's apprenticeship as a poet. His maturity is reached in such classical genres as the Horatian ode and epistle, the elegy and the eclogue. Of these four, the first three can be defined as essentially discursive and epistolary: the poet addresses a friend about a serious problem of death, love or friendship. The eclogue is a more fictional genre, in which nymphs and shepherds reflect in a more distant and stylized way the personal preoccupations of Garcilaso as a lover and poet. The three eclogues, Garcilaso's major works, are analyzed in detail as individual poems.

In taking a new look at Garcilaso's works as a whole, I think that one should try to avoid, insofar as possible, the Romantic tendency to confuse admiration for the heroic man, whom we can no longer really know as a person, with admiration for his poetry, which is still alive and accessible in the form of linguistic and literary structures. The language of Garcilaso, though at times more difficult than it seems, is not very different from the language of Spanish poetry in the present century. Less familiar are the poetic genres, or conventional masks, which give structure to the poet's intention. Lapesa's book has made clear the development of Garcilaso's search for more adequate forms of expression. The present study is a synchronic complement to that view. By grouping Garcilaso's poems, not according to their dates of composition, but according to their types, we can see their interrelationships in another way. This view, however, cannot be radically different from Lapesa's, for Garcilaso's organic development as a poet was closely related to his discovery of new genres.

2. *From Courtly Love to Horace:*
Sonnets and 'Canciones'

T HE works of Garcilaso, as first arranged and published by
his friend and collaborator Juan Boscán, fall into three
groups. The first is a brief and fragmentary *canzoniere* of sonnets and songs. One detail indicates that Boscán considered
the sonnets and songs to be so closely associated with one
another as to form a single group; this detail is that we find
Canción I inserted between Sonnet XVI and Sonnet XVII. [2]
And in themes and attitudes too we find that the songs and
the sonnets are related to one another. But, except for this
one perhaps accidental overlap, there is no attempt to inte-
grate them, as in a complete Petrarchan *canzoniere* such as
Boscán's own, nor has Boscán tried to organize and arrange
the sonnets and the songs as separate groups. We must then
work from the premise that their order is largely accidental,
even though we occasionally find brief sequences of a sort.

Before taking up the sonnets as a group, we should look
briefly at the eight *coplas,* or short octosyllabic compositions.
They are hardly distinguishable from the hundreds of similar
poems found in the *cancioneros* of fifteenth-century and early
sixteenth-century Spain. Their basic themes belong to the tra-
dition of courtly love that was established in European poetry |

[2] Sonnets and *coplas* are numbered somewhat differently in different editions. All editions agree on the first twenty-nine sonnets.
For the sonnets and *coplas,* I follow here the numbering of the Keniston and Rivers editions, but insert in parentheses the number of the
poem in the Navarro edition if it is different. Sonnets XXXIX and
XL are not included in the Navarro edition, and in the Keniston edition
are relegated to an appendix.

by the Provençal troubadours. [3] In Spain this tradition was continued in a witty, rather than a sentimental, vein. It was social poetry, often written upon a public occasion, and was circulated, or read aloud, among groups of courtiers and intellectuals. The lovely but cruel lady is a central figure.

Copla II (I) is said to have been written upon the occasion of Isabel Freire's marriage, but it is a typical stance of the courtly-love poet who, instead of simply accepting the lady's cruel rebuffs as he was expected to by the code, anticipates that she will be punished by the cruelty of someone else. The first stanza reads as follows:

> Culpa debe ser quereros,
> según lo que en mí hacéis,
> mas allá lo pagaréis
> do no sabrán conoceros,
> por mal que me conocéis.

In Copla III (II) the poet promises to cease annoying the lady with his complaints, but expects, emphasizing the paradox, that his silent process of death will speak to her even more eloquently. Similarly paradoxical is Copla VIII, which asserts that no one knows either true bliss or real suffering who has never seen "la belle dame sans merci".

Lighter in tone are Coplas I (VI) and VII, in which the poet jokes about a friend's dancing. Boscán apparently once amazed people by the way he danced at a wedding; with slightly sacrilegious wit, Garcilaso compares this miracle of turning a dance into laughter with Jesus's miracle at the wedding of Cana, when He turned water into wine.

---

[3] For more on this tradition in Spain, see Lapesa (*15*), Green (*37*, pp. 72-122), J. M. Aguirre's anthology of the *Cancionero general* (Salamanca: Anaya, 1971), and Roger Boase, *The Troubadour Revival: A Study of Social Change and Traditionalism in Late Medieval Spain* (London: Routledge and Kegan Paul, 1978).

Sonnets

In the octosyllabic *coplas,* the rhymes come close together, emphasizing witty word-play and antithesis. The shift to the hendecasyllabic, or eleven-syllable, line not only changed the rhythm, but also tended to de-emphasize rhyme. The hendeca-syllable, predominant in Italian poetry since before the time of Dante, became for the Renaissance the modern equivalent of the classical hexameter. In English it is more commonly known as the iambic pentameter, and in French as the deca-syllable. In English and in French, where the last syllable of the line is often a stressed one, it is normal to have only ten syllables in a line; but in Italian and Spanish, in which there is a preponderance of feminine lines with the stress on the penultimate syllable, the norm is eleven. The rhythm is every-where predominantly iambic, that is, tends to stress the even-numbered syllables, but in the first half of the line, inverted feet are common in Spanish. Thus, for example:

cuándo me páro a cóntemplár mi 'stádo.

Here the first foot is clearly inverted: not ∪-, but -∪, if we use the traditional Latin diacritical marks to indicate stressed and unstressed syllables. This longer line with fluctuating stresses (only the tenth syllable must definitely be stressed in every line) introduced into Spanish poetry a new fluidity of rhythm which Garcilaso had developed fully by the time of his major poems. He also developed systems of rhyme-words which were less emphatic, and further de-emphasized them by enjambement, that is, by having a clause run on from one line to the next, with no syntactic break (see *22*).

The sonnet itself was another Italian invention antedating Dante and Petrarch, who brought it to its first great heights of poetic expression. Its structure is based upon an octet, or two quatrains, rhyming ABBA:ABBA, and a sestet, or two tercets, rhyming CDE:CDE or CDC:DCD, or some similar combination of either two or three sets of rhymes. But the rhyme scheme alone does not make a sonnet: it must be reinforced by the syntax, that is, by the interrelationship, whether coördinate or subordinate, consequential or adversative, of minimal units of meaning. Thus every normal Spanish sonnet consists of precisely 154 syllables, with certain coincidences of sound, called rhyme, which begin with the last stressed vowel of each group of eleven syllables. But in addition there is a strong tendency for a syntactic break, at least a comma, to coincide with the line endings and rhymes; stronger breaks tend to occur at the ends of the even-numbered lines in the octet, especially at the ends of the quatrains. These formalistic tendencies, along with the limited number of lines, encourage a condensed epigrammatical tightness of organization. The sonnet has always challenged poets to develop as fully as possible, within this peculiar structure of fourteen lines, the implications of a single thought or brief sequence of thoughts.

Petrarch's sonnets set the basic pattern for sixteenth-century Italian poets, under the leadership of Bembo, and for sonneteers elsewhere in Europe. Garcilaso was no exception. But as Lapesa's study shows, some of his later sonnets might better be called classical than Petrarchan. (Most of his sonnets cannot be dated except by internal evidence and circular reasoning of debatable validity.) In the following pages I shall attempt to group Garcilaso's sonnets according to theme and attitude, commenting in some detail upon the best examples of each group.

Only three of Garcilaso's sonnets are not concerned with his central theme of the sufferings of love. One is an epitaph for his brother, Hernando de Guzmán, who had died of a fever in Naples during the French siege of 1528. This Sonnet XVI ("No las francesas armas odïosas") is a single ironic sentence put into the mouth of the dead man: the first eleven lines emphasize the length of his exposure to the dangers of battle, through which he passed unscathed, only to succumb rapidly, in the last three lines, to malarial death and burial in foreign parts. The compact antithetical structure of this sonnet reflects the concision of the classical epitaphs which Garcilaso no doubt had in the back of his mind as a composite el. In Sonnet XXI ("Clarísimo marqués, en quien derrama") the poet promises the hero praise which will immortalize them both, and describes him as the perfect ideal. Similar praise and poetic tribute is heaped in Sonnet XXIV ("Ilustre honor del nombre de Cardona") upon an Italian woman poet. In both these sonnets the language is hyperbolic, as in love poetry, but there is none of the suffering which inevitably tortures the courtly lover.

The central theme of the remaining sonnets is, quite simply, the suffering caused by frustrated love. Our response to this poetry may be enhanced by a familiarity with the classical and medieval literary traditions which lie behind such poetry, even though, as the poets themselves have always said, anyone who has ever suffered for love will recognize that this poetry has deep roots in the universal human experience. The literary tradition, blending the influence of the Latin poet Ovid with influences of Provençal troubadours of courtly love (see works cited in note 3) and of the Italian poet Petrarch, simply provides a set of conventional devices which the poet may use in his own way. The world of Garcilaso's love sonnets is not strange to the reader of Ronsard and Shakespeare. The basic situation is always something like this: a deliberately cruel, or at least disdainfully indifferent, lady is the most intense, immediate cause of the pain for the helpless and secretly devoted poet. Erotic frustration of this sort is essential to make the poet suffer and sing, or write, of his suffering, analyzing it endlessly, in all of its spiritual aspects. Secondary causes are absence, jealousy or death; these interpose a distance which sometimes attenuates the poet's pain, allowing him further analysis. Greater distance and freedom of expression is achieved when he objectifies the process of love itself, or personifies it as a god. Physical imagery and examples of love drawn from classical mythology allow the poet even greater distance and aesthetic control. Let us examine some of the sonnets which best illustrate these different poetic or rhetorical situations.

The cruel lady in Garcilaso's sonnets seems usually to be located at the end of a steep and desolate mountain road. The poet may address her directly in the polite second person plural ("vos"), as in Sonnet II ("En fin a vuestras manos he venido"), or he may talk about her more objectively in the third person, as in Sonnet I ("Cuando me paro a contemplar mi estado"). The lady herself is sometimes not even mentioned, as in Sonnet VI ("Por ásperos caminos he llegado") and Sonnet XVII ("Pensando que el camino iba derecho"), but the same stark road to desperation clearly implies her all-important, but elusive, presence somewhere in the background.

Perhaps the best poem of this grim group, in which the poet often assumes a deliberately masochistic or self-destructive role, is Sonnet XXXVIII (XXXII):

> Estoy contino en lágrimas bañado,
> rompiendo siempre el aire con sospiros,
> y más me duele el no poder deciros
> que he llegado por vos a tal estado;
>   que viéndome do estoy y en lo que he andado
> por el camino estrecho de seguiros,
> si me quiero tornar para hüiros,
> desmayo, viendo atrás lo que he dejado;
>   y si quiero subir a la alta cumbre,
> a cada paso espántanme en la vía
> ejemplos tristes de los que han caído;
>   sobre todo, me falta ya la lumbre
> de la esperanza, con que andar solía
> por la oscura región de vuestro olvido.

The poet-lover is here enveloped in a damp, windy atmosphere of inhibiting intimidation; he is equally frightened by the lady herself and by the steep, dangerous road leading either away from her or toward her. The final image, in the second tercet, adds a new dimension: formerly guided by the light of hope, he is now plunged into the utter darkness of her "olvido", her deliberate or involuntary ignoring of him. His fear of falling down the steep cliffs is intensified by his not being able to see. This is a nightmare landscape, the very form and content of a psychological impasse.

Quite different is Sonnet XXII ("Con ansia estrema de mirar qué tiene"). Here the lady's disdain, or coy withdrawal,

provokes only sophisticated frivolity on the part of the flirta-
tious poet. The implied elusive relationship between lady and
poet may be essentially similar; but the emotional tone is
radically different, for instead of suffering tragically, the poet
wittily quotes a line from Petrarch, in Italian. |

The traditional courtly rule of secrecy on the part of the
lover is sometimes broken, but the lover sophistically blames,
not himself, but his tongue in Sonnet XXXII (XXXVII: "Mi
lengua va por do el dolor la guía"). In Sonnet V ("Escrito
está en mi alma vuestro gesto") secrecy and blind faith prevail
in the octet; in the sestet the poet declares unambiguously an
absolute devotion of religious intensity:

> ...yo no nací sino para quereros;
> mi alma os ha cortado a su medida;
> por hábito del alma misma os quiero;
>   quanto tengo confieso yo deberos;
> por vos nací, por vos tengo la vida,
> por vos he de morir, y por vos muero.

By "hábito" he means simultaneously a closely fitting
religious garment and that repeated custom which, as in Sonnet XXVII ("Amor, amor, un hábito vestí"), becomes second
nature. Similarly, in the final line, the verb "morir" is used
in two different senses: first literally, and then metaphorically,
implying an excruciating desire.

The eight love sonnets which we have considered so far
all imply confrontation with a cruel lady. Another group, of
nine, is concerned with the suffering caused, not by confrontation, but by physical absence. Absence, if permanent, leads
to despair and death, as in Sonnet III ("La mar en medio y
tierras he dejado") and Sonnet IX ("Señora mía, si yo de vos
ausente"). Alternation between presence and absence may lead
to such metaphorically paradoxical results as freezing when
close to her and burning when far away (Sonnet XVIII, "Si a
vuestra voluntad yo soy de cera"), or it may simply correspond
to the alternation between happiness and painful frustration
(Sonnet VIII, "De aquella vista pura y ecelente"). Absence,

compounding suffering, leads in Sonnet XX ("Con tal fuerza y vigor son concertados") to a suicidal desire for the peace of death, and in Sonnet XIX ("Julio, después que me partí llorando") to sympathetic communication with a friend. The grief of a dog for his absent master is used in Sonnet XXXVII (XXXVI: "A la entrada de un valle, en un desierto") to objectify the presumably even greater suffering of a rational being:

> ...ahora suelta el llanto al cielo abierto,
> ora va rastreando por la vía;
> camina, vuelve, para y todavía
> quedaba desmayado como muerto.

Absence in Sonnet XXVI ("Echado está por tierra el fundamento") may imply the further obstacle of her marriage, but the poet would still masochistically like to see her again. The vacillating rise and fall of hope in Sonnet IV ("Un rato se levanta mi esperanza") leads to the poet's determination to see her again, alive or dead:

> ... muerte, prisiones no pueden, ni embarazos,
> quitarme de ir a veros como quiera,
> desnudo espirtu o hombre en carne y hueso.

Another theme, related to that of absence, is jealousy. The strange relationship between love and jealousy is analyzed in Sonnets XXXI ("Dentro en mi alma fue de mí engendrado") and XXXIX ("Oh celos, de amor terrible freno"). The poet is finally willing to see jealous suspicions confirmed in Sonnet XXX ("Sospechas que en mi triste fantasía").

More serious than jealousy is death, an ultimate mode of absence. But death is not without its transcendental compensations in Sonnet XXV ("Oh hado secutivo en mis dolores"). In the octet, fate is addressed as the destroyer of tree, fruit and flowers, now reduced to ashes which can no longer hear him. In the sestet the entombed lady is asked to receive an interim offering of tears,

> ... hasta que aquella eterna noche escura
> me cierre aquestos ojos que te vieron,
> dejándome con otros que te vean.

The resurrection of the body is here clearly implied, perhaps in an orthodox Christian sense.

One of Garcilaso's most famous, and best, sonnets is vaguer as to the cause of grief: it may be death, absence or simply a change of heart. This is Sonnet X, in which unspecified relics are addressed as the culprits guilty of reminding the poet of lost happiness.

> ¡Oh dulces prendas, por mi mal halladas,
> dulces y alegres cuando Dios quería,
> juntas estáis en la memoria mía
> y con ella en mi muerte conjuradas!
>   ¿Quién me dijera, cuando las pasadas
> horas que en tanto bien por vos me vía,
> que me habíades de ser en algún día
> con tan grave dolor representadas?
>   Pues en una hora junto me llevastes
> todo el bien que por términos me distes,
> lleváme junto el mal que me dejastes;
>   si no, sospecharé que me pusistes
> en tantos bienes porque deseastes
> verme morir entre memorias tristes.

The theme is a familiar one: that present sadness is intensified by the memory of past happiness. But Garcilaso, instead of merely stating the theme as a general abstraction, dramatizes it by accusing certain concrete yet unspecified "prendas" or relics (a lock of hair, as in Eclogue I, perhaps?) [4]

---

[4] This rhetorical device was suggested to Garcilaso by Dido's funeral speech in the *Aeneid,* in which she addresses Aeneas's clothing: "Dulces exuviae, dum fata deusque sinebat" (IV, 651) ("Garments that were sweet so long as fate allowed"). Garcilaso may also have had Boethius in mind, or Dante (*Inferno*, V, 121-23): "Nessun maggior dolore, / che ricordarsi del tempo felice / nella miseria" ("There is no greater grief than to remember a happy time while in misery"). In Jorge Manrique's *Coplas por la muerte de su padre* (ll. 7-9) we

of having deliberately caused his past happiness solely in order to be able to make him suffer more intensely in the present. The first quatrain states the essential accusation; the dual function of the "prendas" is already implicit in the "dulces" and "por mi mal" of the first line. The "prendas" use his own memory as an ally in making him suffer. In the second quatrain the poet emphasizes the irony of his previous innocence: that the same objects in the past should have filled him with one feeling and in the present situation should evoke in him the very opposite feeling. The sestet is less sentimentally nostalgic: here the poet urges the justice of his plea and accusation with hard-boiled logic, antitheses and strangely monotonous rhymes, which change their pattern from verb-endings to adjective only with the very last word of the sonnet, "tristes". The last line, "verme morir entre memorias tristes", after the rigorous reasoning of the preceding five lines, plunges us anew into the sweet melancholy of the octet.

This nostalgic tone of sweet melancholy, characteristic of Garcilaso's most generally appreciated poetry, is not found in the sonnets which we have previously considered, in which the poet directly faces the cruel lady, or bemoans the suffering caused by physical absence or death. In Sonnet X there is no reference at all to the lady herself. Absence or death is implied, but not referred to; the poet's situation depends simply upon the fact that some radical change has taken place. The "prendas" function dramatically in a way that neither the lady nor absence could function, because the "prendas" both witnessed and caused his past happiness and his present grief, and yet they permit an indirection which transforms the poet's anguish into melancholy. In this way Sonnet X represents a very special achievement among Garcilaso's sonnets.

---

find a similar idea: "cuán presto se va el placer, / cómo después de acordado / da dolor". "Cuando Dios quería" seems to have been a cliché, or almost proverbial phrase, in Spanish (see Gil Vicente, *Don Duardos*, l. 823, and Juan Boscán, Canción V). For more details, classical and medieval, see Iventosch's article (*39*).

Also unusual among the sonnets is XXXIV ("Gracias al cielo doy que ya del cuello"), which is a Stoic, or Epicurean, [5] thanksgiving for freedom from the yoke, the stormy sea, the Damoclean sword and the illness of love. This poem is in some respects the reverse of Sonnet X ("Oh dulces prendas por mi mal halladas"), for here the present joy of freedom from love is intensified by the contemplation from afar of those who still suffer under love's tyranny.

We may establish another group of sonnets in which the process of love itself is objectified or personified as the poet's antagonist. For example, Sonnet XII ("No pierda más quien ha tanto perdido") is addressed to the god of love, and love itself is envisaged as a storm at sea. In the quatrains the poet pleads with the god that his obedient service merits respite from suffering: like a shipwrecked sailor, he has hung his wet clothing in Love's temple as a votive offering, with a vow never to go to sea again. But in the tercets the poet again becomes legalistic: his vow had contained escape clauses, specifying that he would not undergo the "same sort" of risk if it was "in his power" to avoid it. The poet now foresees that the next storm will be different from previous ones, and that it will not be within his power to escape becoming involved. The god of love is likewise addressed in Sonnet XXVII ("Amor, amor, un hábito vestí"), this time as the tailor who fitted him with a garment or habit which has become so tight that he cannot shake it off. In other sonnets the process of amorous madness and death in life is described directly, without the rhetorical use of the god as a dramatic device; Sonnets XXXVI (XXXVIII: "Siento el dolor menguarme poco a poco") and XL ("El mal en mí ha hecho su cimiento") are examples of this. Or, instead of the god, a friend and fellow-sufferer is addressed as a sympathetic witness; this is

[5] This sonnet echoes in detail the beginning of Book II of Lucretius's *De Rerum Natura*, the great Latin poem based on the materialistic philosophy of Epicurus. The Stoics and the Epicureans were two different schools of ancient moralistic philosophy; both schools cultivated personal peace of soul, or indifference, in the face of adversity.

the case in Sonnets XXXV (XXXIII: "Mario, el ingrato amor como testigo") and XXVIII ("Boscán, vengado estáis con mengua mía"). Sonnet XXXIII (XXXV: "Boscán, las armas y el furor de Marte") is peculiar in that only in the final tercet are the preceding lines connected with love. The octet is not concerned in any way with love, but with the Christian invasion of Africa in 1535 as a revival of the Roman Empire. (We have a similar allusion to the connection between modern Italy and ancient Rome in Eclogue II, ll. 1545-57.) In the first tercet this leads us to the flames which destroyed the city of Carthage, from which it is an easy step to the flames of love that destroy the poet, especially as he, in the first person, provides the point of view from which the ruins of Carthage are surveyed.

A final group of sonnets are those in which some aspect of love is objectified by means of a simile or a mythological analogy. Sometimes these analogies are referred explicitly and directly to the poet's own case, in the first person; at other times the personal reference is only implicit, if present at all. A peculiarly elaborate example, the only one not dependent upon classical allusions, is an extended simile which makes a single complex sentence out of Sonnet XIV ("Como la tierna madre, que el doliente"); this simile Garcilaso discovered in the poetry of Ausias March. The octet, or vehicle of the simile, describes how an indulgent mother gives her sick child what he cries for, even though she knows that it will provide him with only temporary relief and will in the long run do him greater harm than good. In the sestet the poet-lover (first person) is similarly overindulgent with his sick, mad thoughts, which demand to be fed upon the lady (second person); the result in this case is in effect suicidal.

In Sonnet VII ("No pierda más quien ha tanto perdido") the poet addresses Love as a god, pleading for mercy because of his past sufferings and his devotion to the god; but he knows that, despite vows, he will succumb again. In Sonnet XII ("Si para refrenar este deseo") the poet argues in a single prolonged sentence (the octet is the protasis of a conditional sentence, and the sestet is a conclusion in the form of a

rhetorical question) that if he cannot learn to control himself
by seeing himself suffer, how can he learn to do so from
seeing pictures of the self-destruction of Icarus and Phaeton?
Very similar in rhetorical structure is Sonnet XV ("Si quejas
y lamentos pudieron tanto"), in which the argument is that if
Orpheus's tears for the death of Eurydice had such great
power, then our poet's tears for his own death should certainly
be able to move his lady's hard heart. Sonnet XI ("Hermosas
ninfas que en el rio metidos"), also a single sentence, develops
so fully in the octet the poet's invocation to the nymphs in
their underwater world that the sestet, in which they hear of
his watery tears, seems relatively trivial. As in Sonnet XXXIII
(XXXV: "Boscán, las armas y el furor de Marte"), the significance of the imagery seems to outweigh by far that of the
concluding idea.

In the last three sonnets which we shall consider, the poet's
self or "yo" is eliminated almost completely, leaving the reader
with images that have been almost entirely objectified. In
Sonnet XIII ("A Dafne ya los brazos le crecían") the object
of Apollo's love is tragically dehumanized as she turns into a
tree; he is left caught in a vicious circle, since his tears water
the tree and make it, the cause of his grief, grow bigger and
bigger.

> A Dafne ya los brazos le crecían
> y en luengos ramos vueltos se mostraban;
> en verdes hojas vi que se tornaban
> los cabellos que el oro escurecían;
>   d'áspera corteza se cubrían
> los tiernos miembros que aun bullendo estaban;
> los blandos pies en tierra se hincaban
> y en torcidas raíces se volvían.
>   Aquel que fue la causa de tal daño,
> a fuerza de llorar, crecer hacía
> este árbol, que con lágrimas regaba.
>   ¡Oh miserable estado, oh mal tamaño,
> que con llorarla crezca cada día
> la causa y la razón por que lloraba!

With respect to the octet, we cannot avoid referring to its sources in Ovid's *Metamorphoses*. [6] The *Metamorphoses* provided great stimulation for the sensuous imaginings of Renaissance poets and painters, who with Ovid's help rediscovered a natural physical world of surfaces, of shifting forms and colors. This superficial yet vital world came to replace, in Garcilaso's sonnets, the allegorical abstractions of anguished introspection. Daphne's transformation into a laurel tree is a study of life in the process of change: the eye of the poet, in the preterite verb of l. 3, observes a series of uncompleted events, which are the eight rhyme-words of the octet, all verbs in the imperfect tense. (Ovid had used the historical present, which is less clearly imperfective.) Garcilaso obviously had the Latin text in mind, but his re-creation, especially in the second quatrain ("bullendo", "torcidas"), is the product of an autonomous imagination. The octet, sufficient in itself as a plastic representation of palpitating transformation, is in the sestet seen as subordinate to the plight of the lover Apollo. The final tercet derives, not from Ovid, but from the tradition of witty psychological paradoxes associated with courtly love. Like Sonnet X, Sonnet XIII is a perfect amalgam of two types of poetry, two historical traditions; but the latter sonnet is considerably more impersonal, achieving a neoclassical "aesthetic distance".

We find even greater distance in Sonnet XXIX ("Pasando el mar Leandro el animoso"), a narrative poem based on an epigram by Martial. [7] Leander, swimming the Hellespont to

---

[6] Book I, ll. 548-52: "...torpor gravis occupat artus, / mollia cinguntur tenui praecordia libro, / in frondem crines, in ramos bracchia crescunt, / pes modo tam velox pigris radicibus haeret, / ora cacumen habet..." ("...a heavy numbness seizes her limbs, her tender breast is covered with thin bark, her hair changes into leaves, her arms into branches, her foot, just now so swift, clings to sluggish roots, her head is a treetop...").

[7] Book I, epigram 25: "Cum peteret dulces audax Leander amores, / et fessus tumidis iam premeretur aquis, / sic miser instantes affatus dicitur undas: / 'Parcite dum propero, mergite dum redeo.'" ("When brave Leander was going to his sweet love, and was wearied

visit Hero by night, is caught in a storm and pleads out of
desperation that he be spared long enough to fulfil his amorous
mission. The emphasis seems more sexual than sentimental;
the implications are hedonistic, "all for love, or the world well
lost". But Leander's physical anguish is real, and the reader
is strongly urged, by implication, to empathize with his point
of view.

Sonnet XXIII, "En tanto que de rosa y d'azucena", presents the "carpe diem", or "live for today", theme more explicitly than does Sonnet XXIX. In the Leander sonnet the
poet was present only as narrator; in this sonnet he is present
as the voice who addresses the maiden, in the second person,
and bids her make the most of time. This seems to be disinterested advice: the speaker does not present himself as a
potential lover. But there can be no doubt that the maiden
is being urged to make love.

> En tanto que de rosa y d'azucena
> se muestra la color en vuestro gesto,
> y que vuestro mirar ardiente, honesto,
> con clara luz la tempestad serena;
>   y en tanto que el cabello, que en la vena
> del oro se escogió, con vuelo presto
> por el hermoso cuello, blanco, enhiesto,
> el viento mueve, esparce y desordena:
>   coged de vuestra alegre primavera
> el dulce fruto antes que el tiempo airado
> cubra de nieve la hermosa cumbre.
>   Marchitará la rosa el viento helado,
> todo lo mudará la edad ligera
> por no hacer mudanza en su costumbre.

This is in many ways Garcilaso's most perfectly achieved
classical sonnet. The octet is a series of parallel subordinate
clauses describing the lady's present physical beauty; the first
word of the sestet is the imperative main verb, followed by

---

and hard-pressed by the swollen sea, he thus addressed in misery the
insistent waves: 'Spare me now, drown me when I return.' ")

another subordinate clause in which the lady's future decline is anticipated. The final tercet is a gnomic conclusion, with witty word play upon time's unchanging potentiality for change.

Flowers, or more precisely roses, symbolize the lady's beauty and its evanescence. Her eyes simultaneously inspire and restrain masculine desires. [8] In the second quatrain, the image of golden hair being blown about a long white neck is reminiscent of Botticelli's "Birth of Venus", a painting which Garcilaso may well have seen. In l. 10 "el tiempo airado" or "envious time" would seem to have a secondary meaning of "wintry weather", which leads us into the image of a snow-covered mountain to replace the golden hair and neck of Venus. The sharp edge of the winter wind will always cut down the rose: the monstrously ineluctable machine of time will always cause changes too swiftly.

Canciones

Among Garcilaso's five songs, or odes, we naturally do not find so great a variety as among his forty sonnets. But the range, though more limited, is similar. Canciones I and II, like certain sonnets, are addressed to the "belle dame sans merci" directly, in the second person. In Canciones III and IV the lady is objectified and referred to indirectly. And Canción V, the *Ode ad florem Gnidi,* is quite different: in it the poet pleads with a lady on behalf of another man, his friend. The supreme sufferings of love are the constant theme of the *canciones,* but the dramatic focus, style and imagery vary greatly from poem to poem.

Although the *Ode ad florem Gnidi* has traditionally been grouped with the *canciones,* it was not labeled as a *canción*

---

[8] Herrera introduces a significant, and possibly authentic, variant of l. 4: "enciende al coraçón, y lo refrena". This fits l. 3 very neatly: the lady's gaze, insofar as it is "ardiente", ignites one's heart, but being also "honesto", restrains it. The shift of style in the final tercet, from sensuousness to abstract wit, has been unjustly censured by modern critics who do not understand Garcilaso's synthesis of Hispanic and classical traditions.

in the first edition and clearly differs from the other four in
outer and inner form. Metrically all five are made up of stanzas
in which eleven-syllable and seven-syllable lines are combined
in different rhyme-patterns, but the four songs have syntactically distinct stanzas of from thirteen to twenty lines, while the
ode's stanzas are relatively short five-line units, usually linked
by run-on sentences. Each of the songs ends with a shorter
stanza addressed to the completed song itself; there is no such
"envoi" or farewell at the end of the ode. These differences
of external form can easily be explained historically by reference to the different literary traditions to which the two
groups of poems belong. The courtly tradition of the love song
was founded by the Provençal troubadours and was further
developed by Italian poets such as Petrarch. The ode, on the
other hand, is a classical genre stemming directly from Horace.

In internal form we do not have quite so clearcut a division, for there is considerable variety among the four songs
themselves. Only Canciones I and II closely resemble one
another. In both, the poet's complaints and descriptions of his
situation are a dramatic plea to the lady for mercy. The
psychological self-analysis and the subtle lines of argument
become at times quite complicated and hard to follow, especially for the modern reader unfamiliar with scholastic modes
of thought. But once its severe abstractions are understood,
one finds in this poetry high points of stylized emotional intensity.

Canción I, "Si a la región desierta, inhabitable", begins
by evoking the geographical extremes of desert heat and arctic
cold associated with the lady's cruelty, to which the poet
suicidally submits. He pleads for mercy, however, arguing that
eventually she herself will suffer remorse, which will add a
new dimension to his own suffering. But at present the lady's
sadism exceeds his masochism, a fact which he tries to conceal
from himself out of kindness to her. He sends his song away,
urging it to be as cruelly detached toward him as the lady
and he himself are. It may seem anachronistic to apply to
this poem such modern terms as sadism and masochism, but

this is precisely the vicious circle of self-destruction which the poetry evokes.

Very similar in tone and attitude is Canción II, "La soledad siguiendo". The poet's complaints, addressed to the lady, do not reach her, but return in vain to him. Yet he cannot help continuing his attempts to communicate with her. In his solitude, he calls upon trees and rocks to witness his suffering, to which he fearfully wishes he could resign himself in silence. In his case, however, silence would not indicate alleviation, but rather that his pains exceeded his powers of imagination and expression. She frustrates his attempts at self-deception; his only recourse is to assign himself, with all his suffering, to her. The *envoi* is a veiled threat to say even more unkind things about the lady.

Canción IV, "El aspereza de mis males quiero" (see 27), is closer to Canciones I and II than is Canción III. Although not addressed to the lady or accusing her directly of cruelty, this poem describes a similar torment. Rhetorically, it is addressed to the world at large as a public confession of the cause of his death, which is a madness that uses temporary respites to redouble his torments. The poet narrates the fateful process which has brought him to this situation: his reason had tried to defend him, but quickly succumbed to the onslaught of madness, from which he himself did not want to be saved. The lady's eyes are seen as having planted in him the first poisonous seeds of madness: he now pursues her, but can no longer even see her face, only her distant figure moving and tantalizing him. Her golden hair was the net which trapped him, as Vulcan's net trapped Mars and Venus in flagrant adultery; but although his reason is ashamed, he himself embraces this imprisonment. When he thinks that he can no longer stand the torment, a temporary and illusory relief saves him, only to give way later to redoubled torment. The poet, in his *envoi*, explains that, despite such superficial vacillations, he is in fact led constantly and inexorably to death. Canción IV, much longer than the others, develops fully an allegorical objectification of the process of love. The lady herself is objectified as a pair of eyes, golden hair, a distantly moving

figure, which poison, trap and subject him to the tortures of
Tantalus. Classical mythology and medieval allegory both
function as imagery which gives concrete form to abstractions.
This poem, perhaps because of its hybrid nature, is in many
ways the most powerful of the *canciones*.

The foregoing paraphrases of three *canciones,* which may
seem crude, are justified by the real difficulty which these
poems pose for the modern reader, even if he knows Spanish
very well. Much more accessible are Canciones III and V,
which are more classical in style. In this we see the continuing
effect of the Renaissance, which simultaneously revived the
literature of Classical Antiquity and made more remote and
inaccessible the poetic world of the Middle Ages.

Canción III, "Con un manso rüido", begins with the classical *topos* of the *locus amoenus,* [9] anticipating in this way the
pastoral world of the eclogues. But the poet finds himself out
of harmony with the springtime landscape, for he is imprisoned
upon this lovely island in the Danube. (This sort of historical
allusion is more publicly and concretely autobiographical than
anything in the preceding *canciones.*) While recognizing that
Charles V has the right to imprison him physically, the poet
reasserts that it is only love which can make him suffer spir-
itually, and that in this sense the Emperor is powerless. The
fact that his political career is ruined in fact fortifies the poet-
lover with stoic desperation (ll. 48-52):

> Sepan que ya no puedo
> morir sino sin miedo,
> que aun nunca qué temer quiso dejarme
> la desventura mía,
> que el bien y el miedo me quitó en un día.

---

[9] *Locus amoenus* ("pleasant place") is a handy Latin label des·
ignating a conventional classical landscape, a bower or grove, in which
running water, singing birds and breeze add music to the shade of
trees and perfume of flowers, scattered in the grass. See Ernst Robert
Curtius, *European Literature and the Latin Middle Ages,* trans. Willard
R. Trask (London: Routledge & Kegan Paul; New York: Pantheon
Books, 1953), Chapter X.

A pre-*envoi* stanza is addressed, not to the general public like the rest of the poem, but to the Danube, which besides isolating him from the outside world, paradoxically is his only line of communication with that world. His words in fact must be thrown into the river, where they will probably drown. The *envoi* itself, addressed to the song thus foredoomed, ironically congratulates it upon not having died like other songs in the poet's mouth. In this poem the spiritual sufferings of love are not analyzed, but are taken for granted; public political disgrace and physical imprisonment are seen as easier to bear than the private and intimate anguish of the soul. This new antithesis between the poet's professional career and his inner life reappears in the elegies, but is evaded in the mythic Eden of the eclogues.

The *Ode ad florem Gnidi* ("Si de mi baja lira"), with its playful detachment, frees the poet entirely from the neurotic prison of love. In it he addresses the lady, not as a suffering lover himself, but as the advocate of a third person. His reasoning no longer chases itself obscurely, trapped within the cage of a vicious circle; it develops a classically clear line of argument. Few elements in this poem are directly connected with the medieval cult of courtly love; the only obvious influences, emphasized by the Latin title, are Horace and Ovid, influences which cannot be ignored in a fully adequate reading of the poem. [10]

Given its rational clarity of linear development, Garcilaso's ode can be more simply and accurately summarized than any of the other *canciones*. The first six stanzas (30 lines) form a single sentence: "If I were Orpheus, I would sing not of war and heroes, but of your beauty and the suffering it causes." Stanza seven (ll. 31-5) identifies the sufferer as follows:

---

[10] In addition to the more specialized notes of Wilson (*62*) and Glaser (*34*), see Dunn's important general study (*30*) of Garcilaso's ode, in which the dual meaning of "Gnidi" in the title is explained as referring simultaneously to the Neapolitan district known as Nido, and to Cnydos, the site of an important temple dedicated to the cult of Aphrodite or Venus. Thus the lady is in two ways "the flower of Cnydos".

> Hablo d'aquel cativo
> de quien tener se debe más cuidado,
> que está muriendo vivo,
> al remo condenado,
> en la concha de Venus amarrado.

In addition to suggesting a pun on his friend's name, [11] this stanza gives us a strangely modern and mythological image of love's prisoner as a galley slave, rowing not a boat but a scallop shell, traditionally associated with Venus (and female genitalia), as in Botticelli's famous painting.

In stanzas 8-12 we we find the most direct imitation of Horace (*Odes,* book I, 8): with anaphoric emphasis, the poet states that "for you" the lover has abandoned manly sports, happy songs and his best friends. The lady is urged to be less cruel, and a cautionary tale is abstracted from Ovid (*Metamorphoses,* book XIV, 695-764): Anaxarete, who cruelly drove her lover to suicide, was punished by being turned to stone. The last two stanzas exhort the lady not to tempt nemesis by causing suicide, but rather to inspire poetry of immortal beauty. The whole poem is an elaborately gallant gesture belonging to the salons of Naples, where the Latin classics were well known. This poetry has little to do with the poetic traditions of medieval Spain; it belongs to a new international tradition, that of the Renaissance rediscovery of urbane Horatian sophistication.

---

[11] It seems that Garcilaso's friend was one Fabio Galeota; "galeote" is Spanish for "galley slave", that is, one sentenced to row ("al remo condenado").

3. *Epistolary Discourse: Eleg and Epistle*

ODE, elegies, epistle: these are all classical genres of poetry, and Garcilaso organizes them all in an essentially similar fashion. Each is addressed by the poet, in his own *persona,* to an historically identifiable acquaintance. The dramatic context is thus less conventionally stylized than that of those sonnets and songs addressed to the traditional "belle dame sans merci" of courtly love. The ode in this sense, because it is addressed to a similar lady, but not by her lover, bridges the formal gap between such sonnets and songs, on the one hand, and what I shall call epistolary compositions.

Epistle

In order to define this genre, let us begin with the poem entitled *Epístola a Boscán.* There is no doubt that the poet himself, as he implies in l. 7, intended this poem to be classified as an informal or familiar epistle. His classical models were the *Epistulae* of Horace, which, like Horace's *Sermones,* were written in a colloquial style; the dactylic hexameter, traditionally associated with an elevated epic style, contributes to the modestly ironic tone of Horatian satire, the genre which includes both *Epistulae* and *Sermones* (see 52). In the first line of almost every epistle, Horace mentions the name of the person addressed, as in the heading of a letter; personal details recur most frequently toward the end of the epistle, with something of the effect of a signature. In between, the central topic of moralization is treated in a somewhat more impersonal way, although the tone is still familiarly informal. Thus the rhetorical form of a personal letter frames and permeates the more or less philosophical subject-matter of the Horatian epistle, a well defined genre of versified discourse popular in European literature from the Renaissance until the Romantic movement.

Garcilaso's *Epístola a Boscán,* the first Horatian epistle of Spanish literature, is a perfect example of the genre, even though it is not directly dependent upon any one of Horace's *Epistles* in particular. It is written in blank verse, that is, unrhymed hendecasyllabic lines, a deliberately prosaic colloquial form. It begins with the vocative "Señor Boscán". In the introductory section of the poem (ll. 1-16) the poet remarks that his friendship with Boscán permits a wide range of subject-matter, as well as an easy-going freedom of expression, unhampered by intricate ornamentation such as rhyme. He then playfully gives suspense to the composition, telling his friend that he will not find out where the writer is until he reaches the end of the letter.

The body of the letter (ll. 17-65) begins in a deliberately rambling way. Speculation concerning the benefits of friendship leads back to Boscán, an exemplary friend. The central thought, deriving from Aristotle's *Ethics,* is that the disinterested love which binds two friends is its own reward. Garcilaso develops this thought with an ingenuity and personal introspection that remind us of Montaigne's *Essays.* In fact we realize that, since the eighteenth century, it is the modern essay in prose which has completely replaced the Horatian epistle in verse as the genre best adapted to the informal exploration and exposition of a personal philosophy or moral position.

The final section (ll. 66-85) of Garcilaso's epistle drops abruptly from the level of general observations concerning friendship to jokingly satirical comments on traveling conditions in Southern France, where deception, bad wine, ugly waitresses and high prices seem to abound. We realize that Garcilaso is on his way from Barcelona, where Boscán is, to Naples. The last three lines identify the writer's time and place: October 12, 1534, from the home of Petrarch's love, Avignon. It is precisely the light tone of this casual poetry which captures

the sophisticated urbanity of Horatian humanism, almos
tally lost during the Middle Ages.

Elegies

Garcilaso's elegies are clearly distinguished from his epistle,
but I feel that the differences are not such as to establish a
wholly independent genre. The word "elegy" in classical
literature was rather vague. It seemed most closely identified
with a certain metric form, the elegiac couplet, consisting of
a hexameter followed by a pentameter. As for subject-matter,
the only requirement was that it be plaintive. Propertius was
probably the elegiac poet *par excellence*. His four books of
elegies center on his tortured love for the courtesan Cynthia;
many of them are addressed directly to her, in more or less
epistolary form. Only occasionally is physical death, as distinct
from the metaphorical death of love, the reason for the poet's
lamentation. One of Tibullus's elegies (number 10 of book I)
is a satirical diatribe against war. Another well-known group
of poems written in elegiac couplets is Ovid's *Heroides,* most
of which are letters addressed by famous wronged ladies to
their faithless lovers. Thus we see that the elegy, in its classical
sense, might well overlap with the epistle in rhetorical form.
Each of Garcilaso's elegies is addressed to a friend; in one
case the main subject-matter is love and in the other it is
death. In both, war is attacked as a major source of human
suffering and grief. The metrical form used is *terza rima,* which
corresponds to the elegiac couplet in the same general way
that the blank verse of the *Epístola a Boscán* corresponds to
the loose sequence of hexameters used by Horace.

Garcilaso begins the Second Elegy by addressing Boscán
and identifying his own situation: he is in Sicily with the
Emperor's troops returning victoriously from Tunis. He comments upon their attitudes: in either an open or a hypocritical
way the soldiers all desire to be rewarded for their services.
At this point the poet interrupts his argument in a self-conscious manner (ll. 22-4):

> Mas ¿dónde me llevó la pluma mía?,
> que a sátira me voy mi paso a paso,
> y aquesta que os escribo es elegía.

We see, in this, Garcilaso's somewhat ironic awareness of the differences between the classical genres of discursive poetry; his own pen does not take naturally to maintaining such fine discriminations. He then describes how writing poetry gives variety to his military life.

After this literary introduction, the central portion (ll. 37-144) of the elegy is a discussion of the poet's jealous preoccupation with the probable activities of the mistress whom he has left behind in Naples. Does absence indeed make a lady's heart grow fonder? Not if it is too prolonged. His own love is constant, but he cannot be sure of hers. At this point he briefly apostrophizes war and curses his fate. He cannot be sure which would make him suffer more: his jealous fears, or knowing the worst. He concludes this portion by choosing to deceive himself deliberately with false hopes (ll. 139-44):

> En este dulce error muero contento
> porque ver claro y conocer mi 'stado
> no puede ya curar el mal que siento,
>   y acabo como aquel que en un templado
> baño metido, sin sentillo muere,
> las venas dulcemente desatado.

This image of ancient Stoic suicide expresses in a new way Garcilaso's characteristic note of sweet melancholy, a poetically escapist solution for the violent problems of love, infidelity and death. Suffering, when thus muted, gives rise to beauty.

The concluding section of this elegy, or epistle, brings Boscán back into the foreground. Boscán's stable matrimonial affection is imagined, on a beach near Barcelona, as calming the stormy seas. The poet himself, however, is driven through a world of unrelenting storms from which he cannot escape no matter where he goes. The geographical extremes of the final lines of Elegía II resemble those of the first stanza of Canción I. It concludes abruptly with this line: "Y así diverso entre contrarios muero".

There is hardly an echo of such courtly excruciation in Garcilaso's other elegy, which is his most serious philosophical poem. This is an elegy in the modern sense of the word: it is addressed to the Duke of Alva, Don Fernando, in sympathy and consolation for the death of his younger brother Don Bernaldino de Toledo. Like Elegía II, Elegía I was written in Sicily shortly after the Tunisian campaign. In it Garcilaso drew directly upon the texts of three elegies, two of them only recently published. But his elegy has a unifying structure of its own which assimilates these different Latin and Italian sources. [12]

The theme and structure of the First Elegy is clearly dualistic. The poet recognizes as inevitable, on the one hand, what he presents as the disorderly feminine emotions of human grief and despair in the face of war, death and universal misery on earth. But once these emotions have been indulged in, the poet says, then masculine self-discipline, purgation and heroic emulation can raise us to a heavenly perspective from which earthly suffering seems insignificant, and where all is peace and divine love. The poem moves thus in a transcendental direction. The major break, or shift in emphasis, comes between lines 180 and 181, a break which divides the poem sharply into two parts. But cross-references of an antithetical sort tie the two parts firmly together.

This elegy begins with a long introductory sentence (ll. 1-24) in which the poet states his purpose: to see whether "las musas / pueden un corazón alzar del suelo", that is, whether

---

[12] For an excellent study of the unity of this elegy, see the article by S. F. Rendall and M. D. Sugarmon (*51*). The elegies imitated by Garcilaso were an ancient one often attributed to Ovid (*Consolatio ad Liviam*), a contemporary Latin elegy written by Girolamo Fracastoro for Gianbattista Turriano on the death of his brother, and an Italian elegy written by Bernardo Tasso for Bernardino Rota on the death of his brother.

poetry can raise the heart from earthly grief to heavenly joy.
Earthly grief is then evoked on many levels. We see Don Fernando himself sleeping fitfully in Sicily and grieving as
Lampetia did for her dead brother Phaeton. The poet concedes
that the loss of an ideal brother like Don Bernaldino is
sufficient cause to sadden the most heroic heart. Lines 76-108
are a diatribe against the human condition in modern times of
universal war, exile and loss of loved ones, all to no purpose;
of this Don Bernaldino's premature death is a culminating
example. But already a positive aspect is presented briefly: his
death is a loss for his surviving family and friends, but his
own body is beautiful even in death and seems only to sleep,
"indicio dando del vivir futuro" (l. 129). Nevertheless his
mother and sisters in Spain indulge in a veritable orgy of tears.
Nature is invoked as a source of consolation. The erotic satyrs
and nymphs of Sicily are called upon to comfort Don Fernando.

With this the dark earth-bound forces begin to give way
to an upward movement toward heavenly light. The first step
is one of rigorous stoic self-discipline: Don Fernando is urged
to live up to his heroic reputation, for the "fuerte varón" must
face fortune's ups and downs with constant valor. Even if the
whole universe collapses, the hero should die without fear
(ll. 196-201):

> ... si toda la máquina del cielo
> con espantable son y con rüido,
> hecha pedaços, se viniere al suelo,
>   debe ser aterrado y oprimido
> del grave peso y de la gran rüina
> primero que espantado y comovido.

Only such self-discipline can lead to immortality. Thus
Priam eventually ceased weeping for his dead son Hector; and
even Venus, once she realized that she could not bring Adonis
back to life, decided to return to the joy of love once more.
The poet calls upon Don Fernando to use his reason and his
courage and to set his eyes upon two levels of immortality,
that of fame and that of Heaven itself. With facile syncretism

Garcilaso equates Hercules' fiery apotheosis with the progress of a Christian soul through purgatory (ll. 250-5). The dead Don Bernaldino himself is then envisaged as purged of mortal flesh and seated "en la dulce región del alegría" (l. 261). From this vantage point of eternal reason he views the insignificance of earthly vanities. The same destiny is seen as belonging to Don Fernando also; in a final epilogue, or brief anticlimax (ll. 295-307), the poet promises to sing the Duke of Alva's immortal praises.

· The three epistolary compositions examined in this chapter, together with the ode, constitute a group of Horatian poems of an essentially discursive structure. In Boscán's ordering of Garcilaso's poems, this discursive poetry occupies a central position, coming between his Petrarchan *canzoniere* of sonnets and songs, and his Virgilian eclogues. It is upon the latter, above all, that Garcilaso's reputation as a poet is based.

4. *Nymphs, Shepherds and Heroes:*
Eclogue II

THE pastoral myth is still very much alive, especially in the industrial societies of the Western world. Urban politics, factories and military organizations induce an escapist nostalgia for a more simple life in the country: the lost paradise of mankind's youth, the Golden Age, the Garden of Eden. This mythic world, free of sin and suffering, is associated with innocent sex, moral relaxation and emotional release. In it there is no money, social conflict or hard work, for bounteous nature supplies all of man's simple needs. One clings sentimentally to this oasis of peace and love in the midst of a harshly warring world. In both classical and Biblical literature this myth is often associated with the figure of a shepherd as redeemer. David brings sweet music from the fields into the king's court, and angels announce to simple shepherds the birth of the Messiah. More sophisticated poets such as Theocritus and Virgil wrote idylls and eclogues, or bucolic poems, in which shepherds sing against a mythic Arcadian background of fields and streams. [13]

In the poetry of Garcilaso, the rediscovery of this pastoral world and its evocation in the rhythms of Spanish were a major accomplishment. In so doing Garcilaso found a true voice of his own; his characteristic note of sweet melancholy could best be struck within the nostalgic world of pastoral paradise lost. It was undoubtedly in Naples, the home of Sannazaro, that he was led into the world of Arcadia. *Arcadia*

[13] For a brilliant exploration of this mythic literary world, see Renato Poggioli, *The Oaten Flute: Essays on Pastoral Poetry and the Pastoral Ideal* (Cambridge, Massachusetts: Harvard University Press, 1975).

was the title of Sannazaro's major work, an Italian mosaic of reminiscences from Theocritus and Virgil, from Petrarch and Boccaccio, which brought to life in a new, more self-conscious way the pastoral dream. This work, a mixture of prose and verse, was first published in 1502 and was reprinted frequently during the sixteenth century. Sannazaro had died only two years before Garcilaso's arrival in Naples in 1532.

Garcilaso's first experiment with the pastoral, written after a year or so of being in Naples, was extremely ambitious, though not wholly successful. In this work, his so-called Eclogue II, he tried to write a pastoral work which would be simultaneously epic, tragic and comic. According to the classical hierarchy of genres, based largely upon the social status of the characters appearing within a literary work, the pastoral and the comic were low genres associated with rustic or servants' dialect, whereas epic and tragedy were the genres of aristocratic heroes, in an elevated style. Eclogue II, 1885 lines long, was planned as an encyclopedic work of poetry, echoing the Western tradition from Homer to Ariosto. As such it has been extremely difficult for critics to interpret. [14] But in this eclogue we find the entire range of Garcilaso's poetic virtuosity. And there can be no doubt as to the deliberate care with which he designed the work.

Lapesa's diagram (*15*, 2nd ed., p. 105) shows more clearly than can words the symmetry and formal unity of the Second Eclogue. There are three different types of rhyme scheme: *terza rima, canzone* stanzas, and inner rhyme. [15] A brief prologue in *terza rima* corresponds to an epilogue in the same form. Following the prologue is a choral passage, in stanzas, which corresponds to a similar passage preceding the

---

[14] Coincidentally there appeared, within a five-year period, five substantially independent analyses of the Second Eclogue (*44, 15, 23, 46, 41*). To these should now be added the doctoral dissertation, soon to be published, by Inés Azar (see *26*).

[15] Inner rhyme is found in a series of hendecasyllabic lines, each of which is divided into a seven-syllable and a four-syllable portion: the last word of the first portion rhymes with the last word of the preceding line.

epilogue. Within this framework there are five pairs of similarly corresponding passages. A long narrative in the first
half of the eclogue is divided into two portions, and so is a
long narrative in the second half. Only two passages have no
counterparts: ll. 681-719, in stanzas, a group which seems to
be anomalous; and ll. 766-933, the mathematical center and
emotional climax of the poem. Thus, on the basis of external
form alone, we can perceive that the poem was carefully
planned as a whole.

The Second Eclogue is made up of monologues or di-
alogues; that is, all of its words are put into the mouths of
fictional characters. The poet, as an ultimate narrator, does
not appear upon the scene; the dramatic action is continuous. [16]
Two shepherds, Albanio and Salicio, begin the dialogue by
meeting one another; and two shepherds, Salicio and Nemoroso, end the dialogue by taking leave of one another. Salicio
is thus the linking character, who listens to Albanio's narrative
in the first half of the poem and to Nemoroso's in the second.
The anomalous group of three stanzas concludes the first narrative and introduces the central, and only really dramatic,
portion of the poem, in which a fourth character, the chaste
nymph Camila, is involved. This central portion is a continua-
tion of Albanio's autobiographical narrative, a love story.
Nemoroso's narrative is an epic account of the Duke of Alva's
career.

Given the Duke's status as an historical person, and the
conventions of Virgil's eclogues, critics have attempted to
identify historically the more fictional characters of the poem's
foreground. It would seem reasonable to assume that Salicio
and Nemoroso in the Second Eclogue, as more evidently in
the First Eclogue, represent different aspects of Garcilaso
himself; Salicio ("willowy") is a near anagram of "Cilaso",
and Nemoroso is related to "nemus", an equivalent in Latin
for Spanish "vega". Much more conjectural is the possible

---

[16] For a cogent argument that this poem was in fact intended to
be presented as a court play, see the recent article by Pamela Waley (*60*).

identification of Albanio. The name is clearly related to that of Alva or Alba; but it is hard to see how both of the antithetical narratives can deal with the Duke himself. Somewhat less unlikely is the hypothesis that Albanio is another mask for Garcilaso, since he was closely attached to the Alba family. But much more likely is Lapesa's suggestion that Albanio represents the Duke of Alva's younger brother Bernaldino, who may well have led a more erotic life than did the heroic Fernando. In any case our reading of the poem does not depend upon a correct historical identification of the highly stylized Albanio, in whom we recognize the suffering lover of the courtly tradition in Spanish poetry.

The Second Eclogue begins with a soliloquy by Albanio. His first words describe a spring which is at the center of the bucolic *locus amoenus,* where the entire action of the poem takes place (ll. 1-3):

> En medio del invierno está templada
> el agua dulce desta clara fuente,
> y en el verano más que nieve helada.

The water reminds Albanio of an emotional crisis which took place there; as a symbol the spring functions in somewhat the same ironic way as the "dulces prendas" of Sonnet X or the Danube island of Canción III. The edenic setting, or *locus amoenus,* is evoked with classical details that have been analyzed by Curtius (see note 9):

> El dulce murmurar deste rüido,
> el mover de los árboles al viento,
> el suave olor del prado florecido... (ll. 13-15)

This scene is of vital importance in setting the poem's pastoral tone. And the spring at its center becomes, as we shall see, a theatrical emblem for the action which follows. Albanio's soliloquy upon his conflicting emotions ends as he decides not to run away from the spring, but rather to escape by going to sleep. The *locus amoenus* with its sweet sounds lulls us into the sensuous dream-world of the pastoral myth.

Albanio's brief introduction is followed by the entrance of Salicio upon the scene. He does not see Albanio at first, but sings three stanzas which develop the pastoral theme along the lines of Horace's "Beatus ille". By this I mean that the peacefulness of the bucolic setting is intensified by the introduction of a contrast with the hectic activities of the city, in which one has to cultivate the favor of the powerful and to acquire wealth in the form of silver and gold. The worries and indignities associated with urban life are left behind as one re-enters the idyllically restful realm of the Golden Age. Salicio's song, like Albanio's soliloquy, ends upon the note of sleep; Salicio thereupon discovers Albanio sleeping, and continues with a praise of sleep as one of Nature's great gifts to mankind. Happy individuals profit from sleep by reawakening with a renewed appreciation of their happiness; the sad are fortified by sleep to bear their sadness.

But Albanio awakens with a start from a deceptive dream. Salicio asks him to share his grief by explaining its causes, and this introduces the first section (ll. 143-337) of Albanio's long narrative. He reluctantly describes the happy life which he once led bird-hunting with a girl. He goes into great detail about exactly how they used to capture songbirds, starlings, crows and so on. This passage, an adaptation in verse of a prose passage in Sannazaro's *Arcadia,* has often been criticized as too long and as irrelevant to the main story. Lapesa has explained its length as necessary to balance quantitatively the epic narrative of the second half of the poem. Thematically, the sport of trapping small birds gives substance to the childlike existence of the boy and the girl before sex raised its serpentine head. Diana's forest was a realm of chaste hunters. This paradise, another image of the legendary Golden Age, was lost when simple friendly companionship was corrupted by intense physical desire on the part of Albanio (ll. 320-2):

> El placer de miralla con terrible
> y fiero desear sentí mesclarse,
> que siempre me llevaba a lo imposible.

At this point Albanio breaks off his story.

An interlude spent in dialogue (ll. 338-415) permits Salicio to convince Albanio that he is a sympathetic listener and that Albanio should continue despite the renewed grief which his story causes. Albanio prefaces the second section of his narrative with a brief invocation and continues on a somewhat higher level of emotional intensity. The crucial scene for him was that in which he declared to the chaste nymph Camila that he was in love with her. And this scene took place exactly where he and his listener are now seated, that is, in the center of the *locus amoenus* beside the spring. This spring, or pool of water, played a role in that crucial scene which explains the depth of its significance in Albanio's mind. When Camila asked him whom he was in love with, he replied that she would see the face of his beloved if she looked into the pool. When she looked, of course, she saw her own face reflected there and fled in horror. Thus the "clara fuente", symbol of pastoral peace, became for Albanio an ironic witness to his fall from grace, his loss of Camila.

The rest of Albanio's narrative is a lengthy account of the repercussions upon him of that loss. After four days of lamentation he decided upon suicide; at the top of a cliff he made a farewell speech to the world, which he now repeats for the benefit of his listener. In this speech he apostrophized first Camila, denouncing her cruelty and deafness, and then the gods, the nymphs and the animals of the forest. But when he was about to hurl himself off the cliff, he was blown flat on his back by a sudden blast of wind. [17] Three stanzas of dialogue bring to a conclusion what we may call the first act; Albanio leaves the stage, and immediately afterwards Salicio does.

After a brief pause (there are no stage directions; see *60*) the second act begins with the entrance of Camila, alone. From her soliloquy it is clear that the setting is the same, and that

[17] This story is based closely upon an episode in Sannazaro's *Arcadia*. But whereas Sannazaro's protagonist was rescued from suicide by the tranquilizing appearance of two doves, which inspired hope, Garcilaso's protagonist is morally reprimanded by the violent wind (see l. 661).

she is still a faithful devotee of Diana, the goddess of chastity and hunting. She has been pursuing a wounded stag; in a vague way, this animal, which carries a poisoned arrow buried in his left side, seems to represent Albanio. [18] She is hot and tired; the cool breeze and grass of the *locus amoenus,* evoked once again, are therefore doubly welcome to her. But the spring reminds her of Albanio and their lost companionship; this memory saddens her, although morally she is quite explicit in condemning Albanio's lust. She too, after her soliloquy, escapes into sleep.

At this point (l. 766) Albanio re-enters the scene. He sees the sleeping nymph immediately, but does not recognize her until he gets closer. This encounter is obviously fraught with violent potentialities, both emotional and physical; it marks the beginning of the genuinely dramatic episode which forms the center of this eclogue. From this point until Albanio goes to sleep again (l. 1032) the action is continuous, with dialogue that is much more rapid and colloquial than in the narratives. Such a clearcut change of style, from pastoral lyric to pastoral comic, reminds us that the eclogue was not a purely classical genre.

During the Middle Ages Christmas pageants had provided a different context for shepherds on the stage. These shepherds, called in from the fields to the manger scene of Christ's birth, were not the sentimental idealists of Virgil, urban aristocrats in disguise. The Biblical tradition, as Erich Auerbach has shown in *Mimesis,* was different in this regard from the classical tradition; it gave a more significant function to lower-class characters of a rustic sort. Thus, according to the Christmas story, the first witnesses to the incarnation of God were not wise Oriental kings, but ignorant shepherds. Their surprise at

---

[18] In her study of the classical *topos* of the wounded stag and the spring, María Rosa Lida [de Malkiel] states that "Garcilaso incorporó a su Égloga II como elemento de narración, no como símil, la cierva herida de la *Eneida;* con todo, [...es difícil...] para el poeta evadirse del tema tradicional" (*43,* ed. 1975, p. 60). I am inclined to agree with Inez Macdonald's briefly developed symbolic interpretation (*46,* pp. 8-9).

the angel's news, when dramatized on the medieval stage, was inevitably comic. With their country costumes and dialects, their musical instruments, songs and dances, these non-classical shepherds became associated with slap-stick humor, popular entertainment, low realism. At the end of the fifteenth century and the beginning of the sixteenth, in Spain and Portugal, several able early Renaissance dramatists had made good use of the stock figure of the comic shepherd. The focus shifted from the manger scene to the private lives of country folk, often aristocrats in disguise. Garcilaso was certainly familiar with this tradition, and in particular with the works of Juan del Encina, who had called his shepherd comedies "eclogues" and had even translated Virgil's eclogues into Spanish. This juxtaposition of two different pastoral modes no doubt contributed to Garcilaso's ambitious attempt at literary synthesis in the Second Eclogue.

It is Encina's mode, not Virgil's, which predominates in the central section of this eclogue. After Albanio seizes the hand of the sleeping Camila, and she awakens, they speak phrases taken from everyday Spanish conversation: "¿Qué es esto?", "¿Yo culpa contra ti?", and the ironic "¡Bueno es eso!" of l. 826. And it is not merely the language that gravitates toward the level of comic realism; the action too involves physical violence and trickery. In order to escape Albanio's grasp, Camila begins to exclaim about a lost brooch and promises not to move while Albanio goes to look for it; in fact, as soon as he releases her, she runs away.

This unladylike response to ungentlemanly behavior is the final blow to Albanio's reason. Left alone, he throws himself to the ground with suicidal intentions. When he arises, he is under the strange illusion that he has lost his body. Salicio and Nemoroso enter and observe him, commenting upon his state of mind. The scene of madness which follows is comic and pathetic at the same time; Albanio's illusions reflect metaphorically his psychological preoccupations in a way that does not surprise the modern reader who is aware of the Freudian subconscious. Albanio thinks for a moment that perhaps Camila's body is the one which he has lost, or which

has been stolen from him. He gazes into the spring in his
search and of course sees his own body reflected, but at first
does not recognize it. When he does decide that the reflection
is his own lost body, he tries to rejoin it and addresses it with
longing, like Narcissus in Book III of Ovid's *Metamorphoses*;
and as in the case of Narcissus, the desire seems to be mutual.
Only "exigua prohibemur aqua": "un poco de agua clara nos
detiene." But when Albanio attempts to embrace his image,
he gets wet and angry. When he tries to throw himself into the
pool, Salicio intervenes, only to find himself locked in the
madman's grip. With this the climax of physical violence is
reached; when Nemoroso and Salicio together succeed in
subduing Albanio, who falls asleep once more, the second
section of the eclogue comes to an end.

The third and final section, beginning at line 1032, is
devoted almost entirely to Nemoroso's historical narrative. This
is linked somewhat externally to the Albanio story by the
figure of a magus named Severo, from Alba de Tormes.
Besides having magical powers over nature, Severo has provided Nemoroso with a cure for the madness of love; he may
therefore be able to save Albanio. Severo is easily identified
historically with an Italian friar who from 1522 was the
religious mentor and tutor of the future Duke of Alva. Severo's
cure for love, according to Nemoroso's account, seems to
have been a moral sermon of a traditional sort, with perhaps
an admixture of humanistic stoicism. [19] After this linking introduction there is a brief dialogue between Salicio and
Nemoroso; as previously with Albanio, Salicio once more
urges his interlocutor to tell his whole story against the leisurely
background of the *locus amoenus,* with its murmuring spring
(ll. 1152-3):

> La fuente clara y pura, murmurando,
> nos está convidando a dulce trato.

---

[19] On medical remedies for the madness of love, see Keith Whin-
nom in the introduction to his edition of Diego de San Pedro, *Cárcel
de Amor* (Madrid: Castalia, 1972), pp. 13-16.

Nemoroso, like Albanio before him, prefaces the second part
of his narrative with an invocation addressed to the nymphs
and fauns of the forest. He deliberately lays aside the oaten
flute (l. 1159) of pastoral poetry.

What follows is a brief epic poem (ll. 1154-1828), the
first classical epic to be written in Renaissance Spanish. The
inner rhyme *(rima al mezzo)* is a little awkward. And for the
modern reader in particular, epic poetry is generally a dead
mode. The result of this experiment seems therefore to be
somewhat unsuccessful; but it is still interesting from a
critical point of view. Somewhat elaborate epic framing and
machinery are used to convert contemporary historical events
and people into epic subjects seen from a distance. The classical epic, as a mode or genre, was built upon historical
distance: Homer looked back upon the Trojan War as belonging to a glorious past age of great heroism, no longer possible
in his world. The epic myth, like the pastoral myth, normally
sees perfection in the past; but while the pastoral is deliberately
vague about history, is essentially timeless, the epic depends
upon an historical, or pseudo-historical, perspective, a certain
distance between the narrator and his subject.

Garcilaso, or Nemoroso, will achieve this distance in the
Second Eclogue by using Severo as a scribe to link the narrator to a prophetic realm of heroic deeds graven upon a
crystal urn by the personified Tormes River, who knows
history before it happens. After his brief invocation, the narrator himself virtually disappears. The magician Severo is
reintroduced, to be led by "old Tormes" into the secret
chambers at the source of the river. There the crystal urn, a
classical symbol of a river's source, provides a visual account
of:

> ... las estrañas
> virtudes y hazañas de los hombres
> que con sus claros nombres ilustraron
> cuanto señorearon de aquel río. (ll. 1177-80)

(The past tenses here seem inconsistent with the prophetic
mode of historical distance.) The story begins with Fernando's

great-grandfather, the first Duke of Alva. The narrator constantly uses the device of pretending to interpret visual details: "one could see by his face that he was young", "he was next depicted with bloodstained armor", and so forth. This device is the poet's main way of putting epic distance between himself and a contemporary hero who was actually younger than he. As a result of this deliberate process of reducing Don Fernando's level of actuality or contemporary realism, the poet implicitly integrates him into the same eternal category in which we have met other great heroes of the epic past.

After an account of Don Fernando's immediate ancestors (ll. 1181-1266), his own birth and education are presented with a considerable amount of epic machinery. First we have the Graces attending a lady in childbirth. Next comes a cradle, labeled "Don Fernando", surrounded by the Muses, Apollo, Mercury, Mars and Venus, who parody the Christian rites of baptismal initiation. When his religious tutor is appointed, Severo is amazed to see his own face depicted on the urn; this gives rise to a brief and somewhat humorous explanation by Tormes. Boscán is next recognized as Don Fernando's tutor in the courtly arts. The military training of Mars is balanced by an erotic encounter arranged by Venus. A duel is followed by Don Fernando's marriage to Doña María Enríquez. Thereafter, like young Hercules, the hero is presented with a dilemma: he chooses to follow Virtue rather than Fortune.

The only episode to constitute the central portion of this miniature epic poem is Don Fernando's trip to Hungary to lead Charles V's army against the Turks. This episode begins with the crossing of the snowy Pyrenees (l. 1433) and concludes with the Duke's springtime return to Alba de Tormes. We are told that, once in France, the Duke chose a single companion in order to travel more rapidly; this anonymous character, hardly mentioned, we know to have been Garcilaso himself. Thus the central episode is largely based on the poet's own experience; here he must strive constantly to maintain epic distance. An illness in Paris brings in the figure of Aesculapius. Their crossing of the Rhine recalls Julius Caesar. In Cologne they see a painting of St Ursula being martyred. Finally they join the

Emperor on the Danube. Don Fernando is then seen organizing the troops, establishing a personal rapport with each national group: German, Flemish, Spanish and Italian. The mythological figure of Envy tries to cause him trouble, but the Duke defeats her. The Duke and the Emperor are visited in a dream by the figure of the Danube, who advises them on strategy. The Christian army's easy victory over the Turks is celebrated in a triumph scene, complete with chariot and trophies. The Duke's return to Alba de Tormes and to his wife coincides with the blossoming of spring: Mars' battlefield yields once more to Venus's *locus amoenus*.

After this climax comes an epilogue in which Severo and Tormes discuss the Duke's career. The whole sequence of pictures supposedly refers to future events, the reverse of the historical distance usually imposed by epic poetry. But in this sequence there is a final series of pictures too bright to be seen; these supposedly contain the more distant future events of Don Fernando's life, not yet visible to Severo's human eyes. (These pictures refer, of course, to a non-fictional unknown future, at the time that Garcilaso was actually writing the poem.) With this Severo leaves the river's source and goes home to Alba to record in writing what he has learned of the "future". (We may assume that the Italian friar actually kept an account of his pupil's youthful activities.) These records are what Nemoroso said he himself had seen, and on them he supposedly based his narrative as recited to Salicio.

An epilogue to the Second Eclogue is provided by Salicio and Nemoroso. The former, in two choral stanzas, expresses his admiration for Severo's account of the Duke's career and his conviction that such an able magician will surely be able to cure Albanio's madness. The two shepherds agree to take Albanio to Severo early the next morning. The sun is now setting, with Virgilian smoke rising from the farmers' huts. Salicio takes charge of Albanio, who is still lying motionless, and asks Nemoroso to herd their sheep, promising to prepare their supper if he gets home first. The poem ends with a line of farewell divided between the two interlocutors.

The foregoing account of the Second Eclogue gives us an idea of its rich variety and complexity. It is not easy to read, but several passages are as poetically perfect as anything written by Garcilaso. Where is the essential unity of the poem as a whole? There can be no doubt as to its basic division into three parts: Albanio's personal or lyric narrative, a dramatic section of dialogue and action which involves all four characters, and Nemoroso's impersonal or epic narrative. But what holds these three parts together? Our major clue is the figure of Severo, who links Albanio to the Duke of Alva. What does Severo represent? He is a wise man, a magician, belonging to the same literary family as Shakespeare's Prospero. And his essential trait, as tutor to the Duke of Alva and as counselor to the lovelorn Nemoroso and Albanio, is moral discipline. We realize that this is in fact the theme of the poem. Albanio's problem is uncontroled sexual desire, which leads to a disruption of his relationship with Camila and eventually to violent, degrading madness, of which only Severo may be able to cure him. Don Fernando, on the other hand, has from early youth been under the tutelage of Severo, and he has had no such moral crisis. His life is a model of balanced sanity; he divides his time between Mars and Venus, military service and matrimonial love. Sentimental neurosis is shown to be morally inferior to heroic self-discipline.

So much for the rational and moral structure of the Second Eclogue. Poetically, its epic heroism, associated with the Tormes and the Danube, is inferior to its pastoral sentiment, associated with the mythic spring at the center of Eden. Before Albanio's adolescent fall, the music and clear water of the spring were a symbol of innocence, harmony and peace. Bird-hunting was the sport which provided a basis of child-like companionship between Albanio and Camila. But when lustful desires develop in Albanio, he profanes the spring by using it as a medium of communication with Camila, who flees. Thereafter the spring is an ambiguous symbol for both of them, reminding them simultaneously of their innocent companionship and of how it was destroyed. Bird-hunting is replaced by Albanio's suicidal tears and by Camila's stag-hunting. This strenuously masculine

5. Nature, Infidelity and Death:
Eclogue I

THE Second Eclogue was an ambitious experiment; the First and Third Eclogues are finished works of art. They are each less than one quarter as long, and are much more simply coherent. There is little admixture of dramatic or narrative impersonality; the poet in his own *persona* introduces each poem and, in a less obvious way, assumes the role of a lyrical shepherd. The First Eclogue is relatively naive in its sentimental directness; the Third, written later, is more sophisticated, more purely aesthetic. But both achieve a level of classical perfection and integration which the Second Eclogue would never lead one to expect.

The First Eclogue consists of thirty *canzone* stanzas which are arranged in a clearcut pattern. [20] The first three stanzas are introductory; in them the poet announces his theme and addresses the Viceroy of Naples, to whom the poem is dedicated. The next stanza sets a pastoral sunrise scene and introduces the first shepherd Salicio; his song of complaint denouncing the unfaithful Galatea occupies the twelve stanzas that follow. After Salicio's song there is one transitional stanza, introducing the second shepherd Nemoroso; his elegy for the dead Elisa likewise occupies twelve stanzas. A final stanza describes the sunset and the shepherds' exit.

[20] The rhyme scheme and pattern of heptasyllabic and hendecasyllabic lines (indicated by small and capital letters respectively) are as follows: ABCBACcddEEFeF. There are only two exceptions, occurring near the beginning of Nemoroso's song: l. 263 has seven rather than eleven syllables, and the following stanza (ll. 267-81) has fifteen rather than fourteen lines, rhyming in the following pattern: ABCBACcddEEFGfG.

sublimation on the part of the girl is clearly symbolic of her moral superiority to Albanio. But the wounded deer, sometimes associated in literary tradition with Dido's desperate love, is relentlessly pursued by the virginal Camila, who is unaware that the deer is leading her back to Albanio; consciously she clings to the cult of Diana, chaste goddess of the hunt.

The symptoms of Albanio's madness, when precipitated by Camila, are more explicitly symbolic of his moral crisis. He imagines that he has lost his body and is free to die or to move wherever he likes. He confuses his own body with Camila's quite different one, recalled in his memory. And he violently attacks the reflection of his body in the spring, as well as his friend Salicio, when the latter tries to restrain him from drowning himself. This entire psycho-poetical world of suicidal sentiment exemplifies the fertile explorations of Garcilaso's pastoral imagination.

I.	3 dedicatory stanzas	st. 1-3
II.A:	1 stanza introducing Salicio	st. 4
	12 stanzas of Salicio's song	st. 5-16
B:	1 stanza introducing Nemoroso	st. 17
	12 stanzas of Nemoroso's song	st. 18-29
C:	1 concluding stanza	st. 30

The symmetry of this poem is evident even to the most casual reader; it consists essentially of two substantial songs set within a slender framework, with a preceding introduction or prologue (see especially *24, 49* and *63*).

In the first six lines of the introduction the poet announces what he proposes to write about:

> El dulce lamentar de dos pastores,
> Salicio juntamente y Nemoroso,
> he de cantar, sus quejas imitando;
> cuyas ovejas al cantar sabroso
> estaban muy atentas, los amores,
> de pacer olvidadas, escuchando.

The poet thus separates himself from his two fictional shepherds, but his words will be theirs: he simply records their lamentations in verse.

Following these six lines, Garcilaso addresses the Viceroy directly and emphatically; it is in the title of the poem that the Viceroy is clearly identified, but the poet's description of him as a ruler, warrior and hunter, and his use of the adjective "albano", would make it possible for us to guess his identity in any case. Garcilaso promises Don Pedro de Toledo that when he has sufficient leisure, he will write heroic poetry concerning him; but meanwhile, until he can perform this duty, he asks permission to descend from epic to pastoral verse, and invites the Viceroy to listen.

After this apologetic dedication, the poet sets the scene in stanza 4. The sun comes up out of the sea and lights up the mountains (are we on the eastern coast of Spain, toward Italy?). Salicio, lying on the grass under a tree, begins his song in harmony with a nearby trickling stream, addressing complaints to his cruel lady as though she were present. The rhetorical situation is the same that we have seen before in several sonnets and *canciones:* the courtly lover laments his lady's cruelty. But in this case a pastoral setting, representing the natural order uncorrupted, is harmonized with the poet's song; and he accuses her quite specifically of an infidelity which violates that natural order. The final line of each stanza, except of the last, is a refrain which sobbingly ebbs and flows: "Salid sin duelo, lágrimas, corriendo".

> ¡Oh más dura que mármol a mis quejas,
> y al encendido fuego en que me quemo
> más helado que nieve, Galatea!

The tone of this beginning (ll. 57-9), along with the name Galatea, reminded the humanistically educated reader immediately of the pitiful love song of the Cyclops Polyphemus. Theocritus, the major pastoral poet of Greek literature, had devoted almost all of his Idyll XI to the Cyclops' song, in order to demonstrate that poetry was the only remedy for unhappiness in love. In this first version there was no rival or jealousy; it was simply a question of a monstrous shepherd, ugly but wealthy, and his unrequited love for an inaccessible sea-nymph. More familiar than this Greek source was Ovid's version in the *Metamorphoses* (Book XIII, ll. 738-897). Here the story was told by Galatea herself, who had been in love with Acis. She described the monster and the scene in which, while she and Acis were in hiding and making love, the Cyclops had sat upon the beach and sung his song. She quoted the song in full; similar in many details to the text of Theocritus, it ended on a ferociously jealous note and led directly to the destruction of Acis by Polyphemus. Garcilaso expected his reader to recognize this tradition which he was elaborating upon, in quite a different way, in Salicio's song. He also expected his friends to recognize an autobiographical aspect of the poem: Salicio's reproaches to Galatea correspond in some way to Garcilaso's own attitude toward Isabel Freire when she married Don Antonio de Fonseca. In this context it is Fonseca, and not the singer, who is viewed as the ugly monster.

All of this is background for a fuller understanding of Salicio's song. But the song itself is essentially independent of this classical and autobiographical background; it is dependent upon its own inner principle of thematic unity. After his first stanza, in which he declares to Galatea his suffering and shame at being forsaken, Salicio introduces his main theme, the harmony of nature. In his second stanza, which is the sixth stanza of the poem as a whole, the shepherd describes how the rising sun governs the daily activity of birds, animals and people. The normal human being, in the morning, begins anew his usual occupation, "do su natura o menester l'inclina". Only Salicio himself is excluded from this natural order, for he laments constantly, regardless of the time of day. In stanza 7 Galatea is accused of being the ultimate source of this disharmony, by having broken her faith to him. Such perjury, causing the death of a friend, deserves punishment from above; but nothing is as it should be, where Galatea is concerned.

In stanza 8, the first six lines describe the past love which kept Salicio in apparent harmony with the landscape; but even then her falsehood, like the proverbial snake hidden among the flowers, was ominously foreshadowed by the sinister voice of the crow. The following stanza describes a nightmare which similarly should have warned him: he dreamt that when in midsummer he took his sheep to the Tagus to drink, the waters flowed away, and he ran after them, hot and thirsty. Thus Salicio reinterprets his past happiness as based upon illusion and self-deception.

Stanza 10 begins with a rhetorical series of five questions, reminiscent of one of Horace's poems (Book I, Ode v): Salicio asks Galatea with searching details whom she is embracing now. Then her infidelity is characterized by classical metaphors comparing the woman to a vine: the ivy has been ripped from one wall and attached to another, the grapevine is intertwined with the branches of another elm tree. So unnatural a violation of an intimate symbiotic harmony is enough to cause grief in any human heart. The precedent set by Galatea's infidelity is seen in stanza 11 as a threat to the entire order of the world, and as a cause of fear to lovers everywhere. The emphasis then

shifts from her broken vows to the unnatural difference between
Galatea and her new lover; in stanza 12 her new union is
compared to the union of lamb with wolf or of bird with
snake. [21] These similes mark the climax of Salicio's main theme;
he deplores the destruction of natural harmony, or the introduction of unnatural discord into what should be an ideal world.
This is clearly related to the essential pastoral myth: Eden
somehow bears within itself the poisonous seeds of its own
destruction.

A secondary theme is developed in stanza 13. If the new
lover is an unnatural mate for Galatea, Salicio does not hes-
itate to praise his own wealth, musical ability and handsome
figure. He has simply been unfortunate, the victim of an
irrational "ventura"; as he continues the argument in stanza 14,
Galatea can have had no possible objective reason for aban-
doning Salicio.

A final complaint against Galatea's unnatural cruelty fills
stanza 15, which is Salicio's penultimate, ending with his last
repetition of the tearful refrain. In this stanza all of nature is
seen to sympathize with Salicio: stones soften to his tears,
trees lean toward him, birds change their songs to match his
sadness, and beasts stay awake to listen to his lament. Thus
all the realms of nature, mineral, vegetable and animal, are in
harmony with him; only she maintains her unnatural cruelty,
refusing even to look at him.

In Salicio's last stanza he surrenders, in an anticlimax of
self-sacrifice. Convinced of her obdurateness, he will withdraw
and leave the *locus amoenus* to her and her new lover. He
describes the setting briefly; there is a hint that his generous
withdrawal may make possible the re-establishment of natural

---

[21] There is a complex literary tradition behind these violent unions,
or "impossibilia". A primary influence is Virgil (Eclogue VIII, ll. 26-8):
"Quid non speremus amantes? ..." ("What strange things are not in
store for us lovers?"). This is combined with a passage from Ovid
(*Ibis*, l. 44) and with certain Messianic passages from the book of
Isaiah (xi. 6-8 and lxv. 25), specifically mentioning the wolf and
the lamb.

harmony, a new, though temporary, paradise of love. Without the usual refrain, Salicio's song ends rather abruptly. It is the transitional stanza that provides a conclusion by describing his now inarticulate tears, to which all of nature, represented by the mountain and the nightingale, responds in sympathy.

The same transitional stanza introduces Nemoroso's song as something on a higher level, to be imitated, not by the unworthy poet, but by the Muses themselves. We are in fact shifting from the indignant accusations of a jealous lover to the elegiac lament of a bereaved one. (Nemoroso's song corresponds to the First Elegy as Salicio's does to the Second.) Nemoroso's opening lines set a tone of tranquil beauty by addressing the waters, trees, grass, birds and ivy as witnesses to his past happiness and present grief (ll. 239-44):

> Corrientes aguas puras, cristalinas,
> árboles que os estáis mirando en ellas,
> verde prado de fresca sombra lleno,
> aves que aquí sembráis vuestras querellas,
> hiedra que por los árboles caminas,
> torciendo el paso por su verde seno ...

Nature here is a complex of closely interrelated elements: the grass is shaded by the trees, the birds scatter their songs like seeds, the trees are reflected by the water and besieged simultaneously by the ivy. This harmoniously interwoven complex, like the "prendas" of Sonnet X, has ironically ambiguous associations, past and present, happy and sad. Whereas Salicio's stanzas are neatly contained by their refrain, Nemoroso's first long sentence runs on over from his first stanza into his second (stanzas 18 and 19). And, with conscious artistic control of form, Garcilaso allows Nemoroso's first surging emotions to break the metric pattern in stanzas 19 and 20 (see note 20), a pattern which is elsewhere rigorously maintained.

It is in stanza 19 that the cause of Nemoroso's grief, his indictment of fate, is first stated (ll. 259-62):

> ¡Oh miserable hado!
> ¡Oh tela delicada,

                          antes de tiempo dada
                    a los agudos filos de la muerte!

Just as Galatea's infidelity was viewed by Salicio as unnatural,
so Elisa's premature death now causes Nemoroso to protest
against what seems unjust and unnatural in nature itself. However, he accuses not nature but fate: premature death is clearly
opposed to natural harmony and fulfilment. This is the attitude
expressed in the First Elegy too, ll. 76-7 ("¡Oh miserables
hados!"), and ll. 97-102, where Don Bernaldino's equally premature death is attributed to an unjust "enemiga / del humano
linaje, que envidiosa / coge sin tiempo el grano de la espiga".
    Stanza 20 begins with the rhetorical "ubi sunt?" question:
where are Elisa's eyes, her hands, her golden hair and graceful
neck? The response is another indictment of the unnaturalness
of her fate: all this feminine beauty is now confined to the
cold, hard prison of earth. The anomalous extra line appears
immediately after the series of rhetorical questions, and its
rhyme leads to this stanza's final word, "tierra". The following
stanza begins with another rhetorical question, addressed this
time to Elisa herself: who could have anticipated such a radical
change from happy companionship with her (first three lines)
to solitary loss of love (next three lines)? Again unjust fate
("el cielo") is seen to be the source of Nemoroso's suffering: fate has bound him to life, his dark prison (ll. 292-5):

                    Y lo que siento más es verme atado
                    a la pesada vida y enojosa,
                        solo, desamparado,
                    ciego, sin lumbre, en cárcel tenebrosa.

Nemoroso's next four stanzas (stanzas 22-5) objectify and
universalize, by myth and simile, the meaningless horror and
grief into which Elisa's death has plunged him. This death has
blighted the world of nature itself and lies like a curse upon
the land. The cattle no longer find enough grass, and the
farmer's harvests are no longer plentiful; weeds and thorns
have overwhelmed the wheat and flowers of the fields. In this
way Elisa is converted mythically into a fertility goddess, whose

death has brought sterility to the land. And, with an ironical touch reminiscent of Sonnet XIII, Nemoroso's tears water the weeds and make them grow.

Stanza 23 is a formal simile ("como ..., tal es..."), in which nightfall and the rising of dark and fearsome shadows are evoked and compared to Elisa's death; but here the alternating rhythm of night and day leads the poet to anticipate an eventual sunrise, implying a reunion with his beloved. A more elaborate simile is developed, epic-style, in the two stanzas that follow. Stanza 24 evokes in detail the grief of the nightingale whose young have been stolen by a cruel farmer and who sings lovely laments all night long; in the next stanza Nemoroso compares himself to the bird, and death to the cruel farmer. Then, after apostrophizing death, he adds these lines of self-analysis (ll. 348-51):

> El desigual dolor no sufre modo;
> no me podrán quitar el dolorido
> sentir si ya del todo
> primero no me quitan el sentido.

In stanza 26 Nemoroso describes a ritual by which he temporarily relieves his grief. He carries with him always, like a religious relic, a lock of Elisa's hair, wrapped in a white cloth. First he unties the hair and weeps over it; then, with burning sighs, he dries the strands and counts them one by one, as though they were the beads of a rosary; finally he puts the hair together and ties it up again. After this intense emotional exercise Nemoroso is allowed to rest for a while by the subsiding rhythm of grief.

But immediately, in the following stanza, cruel memories assault him again: he imagines the dark night of Elisa's mortal labor pains, and he hears her lovely voice, now stilled forever, appealing to the goddess of childbirth for aid in her travail. In the final line of the stanza, as though evoked by sympathy, Nemoroso's own voice addresses the goddess Lucina in accusing tones. This line introduces a series of bitterly rhetorical questions which, with a final exclamation also addressed to Lucina, fill the following stanza.

In the figure of Lucina, goddess of childbirth, we have the final personification of that arbitrarily destructive force in nature which Nemoroso had previously referred to, more abstractly, as fate or death. Like these, she is characterized as cruel and inexorable. But the mythological *persona* of Lucina is quite ambiguous. She was traditionally identified both with the chaste huntress Diana and with the Moon, hopelessly in love with the shepherd Endymion. These ambiguities allow Nemoroso a special sort of irony in his questions: was the goddess neglecting her childbirth functions because she was too busy hunting animals or gazing upon the sleeping shepherd? His final, double question implies a more serious accusation: how could the deity of birth and life cruelly refuse to save from inert death such a beautiful young woman, and how could she simultaneously condemn to grief a vital young man, always vigorously devoted to the hunt? Nemoroso's last bitter exclamation accuses the goddess of being ungrateful to him for his sacrifices as a hunter; with deliberately cruel laughter she lets him see his beloved die (ll. 392-3):

> ¡Y tú, ingrata, riendo
> dejas morir mi bien ante mis ojos!

After this bitter climax of accusation, which denounces the imperfection of the natural world in which death exists, Nemoroso in the last stanza of his song turns his eyes up to Heaven, the seat of immortality. This is the same transcendental realm, Platonic and Christian, [22] which we have seen before at the end of the First Elegy. Here Nemoroso addresses his prayer to the blessed Elisa, now eternally unchanging, asking her to intercede for him in Heaven, to hasten his death and reunion with her. Once liberated from the prison of natural life, he will rejoin her in the sphere of Venus, where, hand in hand, they

---

[22] See Otis H. Green, "The Abode of the Blest in Garcilaso's *Égloga Primera*", *Romance Philology*, VI (1952-3), 272-8. But it is clear that in his two descriptions of Heaven, Garcilaso avoided being explicitly Christian or pagan: he exemplifies Renaissance syncretism in the best sense.

can find a new pastoral world that is not threatened by the loss and separation of death. This stanza is Garcilaso's ultimate metaphysical sublimation of the pastoral world; love becomes eternal in a world free of suffering and death (ll. 394-407):

> Divina Elisa, pues agora el cielo
> con inmortales pies pisas y mides,
> y su mudanza ves, estando queda,
> ¿por qué de mí te olvidas y no pides
> que se apresure el tiempo en que este velo
> rompa del cielo y verme libre pueda,
>   y en la tercera rueda,
>   contigo mano a mano,
>   busquemos otro llano,
> busquemos otros montes y otros ríos,
> otros valles floridos y sombríos
> donde descanse y siempre pueda verte
>   ante los ojos míos,
> sin miedo y sobresalto de perderte?

With the climax of this stanza, certainly one of Garcilaso's finest, Nemoroso's song comes to an end. The final stanza of the First Eclogue is a muted coda, a classical diminuendo, in which sunset gilds the clouds, shadows fall from the hills, and the shepherds, as though awakening from their dream-world of love, lead their sheep slowly homeward. The sunset of the concluding stanza 30 corresponds to the sunrise of stanza 4, emphasizing the symmetrical unity of the poem as a whole.

Each of the two shepherds' songs has its own thematic or situational unity. Salicio complains of Galatea's infidelity and accuses her of not being in harmony with nature. Nemoroso complains of Elisa's premature death as unnatural too; death in fact seems to be a flaw in nature itself, and must be transcended supernaturally. But what, in addition to the setting or framework, unites the two songs to one another? The lyrical situations which they evoke are two of the basic contexts of suffering in love. Infidelity and death: implicitly we are asked to compare and to contrast these two evils which destroy lovers' happiness. Infidelity exists on a purely human level; it is a violation of natural harmony, and it puts an end to the human relationship within which it arises. Death comes some-how from outside the human world; thus, although it would seem to be inevitable, one lover has not forsaken the other, and their love can survive in another world. Thus Nemoroso's grief gives rise to a spiritual beauty from which Salicio is cut off. It is this contrast, within an idealistic theory of love, which relates the two songs to one another.

6. *The Pastoral Paradox of Natural Art: Eclogue III*

THE First Eclogue, in its sentimental and metaphysical directness and simplicity, may be criticized for falling into the pathetic fallacy (projecting purely human feelings into the impersonal universe). The Third Eclogue avoids any such criticism by maintaining a quite unsentimental aesthetic distance, as certain critics have argued. [23] Its more complex formal symmetry is mathematically precise. Its forty-seven *ottava rima* stanzas, each syntactically self-contained, fall neatly into three main groups: a very clearly delimited central group of twenty-one stanzas (ll. 105-272) devoted exclusively to a description of the nymphs' embroidered fabrics of gold and silk, preceded by thirteen introductory and followed by thirteen concluding stanzas. Within each of these three main groups one may distinguish equally clear-cut but less symmetrically arranged subgroups:

I. 13 introductory stanzas
- A. 7 dedicatory stanzas — st. 1-7
- B. 6 stanzas describing setting, and emergence of nymphs — st. 8-13

II. 21 central stanzas
- A. 2 introductory stanzas concerning tapestries — st. 14-15
- B. 18 central stanzas — st. 16-33
  - a. 3 stanzas on Orpheus and Eurydice — st. 16-18

[23] See especially Paterson (*50*), Rivers (*53*) and Spitzer (*59*). The pages which follow are an adaptation of the second of these studies.

The general introduction consists of seven dedicatory stanzas addressed to the "ilustre y hermosísima María", and of six stanzas describing the setting and the preliminary action of the nymphs. The conclusion consists of four transitional stanzas, which introduce the distantly heard shepherds; the eight stanzas of their antiphonal song; and one final stanza in which the shepherds are heard to be on the verge of appearing, and in which the nymphs are seen with neat evasion to disappear silently beneath the waves. The central group of twenty-one stanzas has its own inner introduction and conclusion, of two stanzas and of one respectively, in which the material and artistry of the embroidered fabrics are analyzed; the remaining eighteen stanzas consist of three subgroups of three (the ancient myths of Orpheus and Eurydice, Apollo and Daphne, and Venus and Adonis) and one of nine (the "modern" pastoral myth of Elisa and Nemoroso). These nine stanzas are clearly the climax of the central section of the poem, and of the poem as a whole. An artfully asymmetric symmetry leads us to focus our attention upon the death of Elisa; this scene, as we shall see, embodies the poet's most significant intuitions concerning nature, art, and imitation in poetry.

The hyperboles of the dedication to María are no doubt consciously conventional; they typify the language of courtly love addressed with careful propriety ("voluntad honesta y pura") to a lady of great social prestige. Garcilaso's platonic devotion and the fame of her beauty and mind will together survive death itself.

Garcilaso explicitly addresses himself to the question of conventionality in poetry. He asserts that, despite the obstacles which Fortune throws in his way, he will eventually write immortal poetry about the lady; meanwhile he offers her a modest trifle, free of rhetorical ornament, written in the natural language of the innocent heart. We recognize at once the trademarks of the pastoral convention: the ambiguous modesty of the well-read poet who deliberately assumes the rustic role of the shepherd playing clumsily on his crude pipes and making up with natural sincerity for what he supposedly lacks in artistic technique. The artifice of sincerity is very artful indeed, and inevitably it raises the fundamental question of the relationship between art and nature, of sophistication versus simplicity; the pastoral poet of the Renaissance is consciously having it both ways, knowing all the while that in actuality, as Cervantes was later to declare, most shepherds are thieving scoundrels, brutalized — not refined — by solitude and contact with nature. Yet the pastoral myth has a universal validity, for man will always dream of the legendary Golden Age, an uncorrupted natural world in which human beings are more simply and authentically human; it is this ideal make-believe world, in which art provides a second and better nature, that Garcilaso, with gentle irony, invites María, and the reader, to enter.

In each of his eclogues Garcilaso takes care to plunge the reader deeply into the almost mystical atmosphere of an eternally Edenic quiet shady spot consisting normally of at least one tree, soft grass, and a trickling spring or brook, with perhaps some bright flowers, the song of birds, and a gentle breeze. Garcilaso's *locus amoenus* is in each case deeply rooted in the mythic world of this pastoral tradition; in the Third Eclogue this world is evoked more poignantly than ever, and at the same time is given a familiar geographical location upon

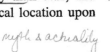
myth & actuality

the banks of the Tagus near Garcilaso's native city of Toledo, beginning with stanza 8 (ll. 57-64):

> Cerca del Tajo, en soledad amena,
> de verdes sauces hay una espesura
> toda de hiedra revestida y llena,
> que por el tronco va hasta el altura
> y así la teje arriba y encadena
> que'l sol no halla paso a la verdura;
> el agua baña el prado con sonido,
> alegrando la hierba y el oído.

For the definitive stylistic analysis of this stanza and the four that follow, one can only return to the brilliant pages of Dámaso Alonso, in which Garcilaso's delicate control of word-order, rhythm, rhyme, and enjambement are shown to contribute immeasurably to an atmosphere of voluptuous sensuousness; the reader finds himself in a world of shade and water, of light and color perceived at noon, of nymphs rising from the depths of the river to spend a pastoral siesta among the trees. Nature itself is represented here as peculiarly artificial, as "natura artifex"; the ivy weaves and enchains the treetops, thus anticipating the nymphs, who will similarly weave their tapestries. This fabric of ivy provides a natural parasol, an "agradable frío", which will protect the nymphs against the ravages of the desiccating noonday sun, "el sol subido en la mitad del cielo", with its overtones of the threatening midday demon. Within the shelter of this willow grove, running water performs simultaneously a dual function, one natural and one artificial: it bathes the greensward with sound, delighting the grass with natural irrigation and the human ear with that natural music so skillfully cultivated by the Moorish builders of gardens in Toledo and Granada. This whispering music is soon echoed by that of the bees ("en el silencio sólo se escuchaba / un susurro de abejas que sonaba"), as it will later, at sunset, be echoed by the distant songs of the shepherds.

Little wonder that the imaginary girl-like inhabitants of the river's depth are attracted to this *locus amoenus*. The nymphs here are not simply taken for granted as stock figures of classical mythology, but are rather re-created visually in the mythopoetic imagination of a great Renaissance poet. Passages of this sort indicate the profound importance of Ovid and of Italian mythological paintings in the formation of Garcilaso's mature aesthetic sensibility. The poetic reality of these nymphs indicates the extent to which Garcilaso was capable of experiencing imaginatively a variety of pantheism in which the human artist collaborates with "natura naturans, natura artifex", in creating beings which belong at the same time to the natural and to the human worlds, like the feminine curves of ripples on the river or the metamorphosis of slender maidens who turn into graceful trees.

In the sixth and last stanza of the section describing the emergence of the nymphs, after they wring out their hair and scatter it over their lovely shoulders, they finally take out, from somewhere (are they really nymphs, or young ladies in a salon?), their handwork and begin embroidering. This is the first mention made of the "telas"; the first two stanzas of the poem's central section are devoted to an explicit analysis of these fabrics.

The main emphasis in stanzas 14 and 15 falls upon the process of converting the raw materials of nature (the legendary grains of gold in the Tagus, green leaves, and shellfish juices) into artistic materials: golden threads and silken yarns dyed various colors. Garcilaso is, in fact, quite ingenious in emphasizing the pastoral source of silk in a way which parallels the piscatorial sources, established in classical literature, for gold and for dye; all of these materials are, of course, readily accessible to his amphibious nymphs. There is an analogy between the nymphs' creative activity and that of the poet himself; such words as "convenía" and "estilo" belong to the poetic precepts concerning stylistic decorum. Just as the ivy weaves shade in the treetops and the nymphs weave their pictures of silk and gold, so the poet is weaving his highly poetic fabric out of common Spanish words. For, beyond the technological process of manufacturing golden and colored threads, we have in the second half of stanza 15 a significant reference to the artistic process, the "artificio", by which the nymphs convert these threads into pictorial works of art, comparable to the "tabulae" of two famous Greek painters.

The eighteen stanzas which follow, as has already been noted, are divided into three groups of three and one of nine. First we see depicted in two scenes the death and the second loss of Eurydice, with a final scene in which Orpheus complains to the lonely mountain in vain. Next, Apollo turns from hunting to the pursuit of Daphne, but her arms become branches, her hair leaves, and her feet twisted roots; it is the bereft lover who again occupies the final scene. Thirdly, a boar and a young hunter attack each other; Adonis, mortally wounded, is in the final scene embraced by a desperate Venus. This secondary plane of mythological pictures is related to the world of the *Metamorphoses* in a more explicit way than is the primary plane of the nymphs who weave the tapestries. In these familiar stories (for Orpheus Garcilaso draws on Virgil's version as well as on Ovid's) the transformations are not escapist fantasies or playful tricks of the imagination, for the ultimate of nature's transformations is seen to be that of death, when the beloved person disappears as a mere shade in "el triste reino de la escura gente", or turns into an unfeeling piece of wood, or stains the white flowers with red blood and becomes a body that no longer breathes. Far from being an act of collaboration between man and nature, such transformations as these are a profound challenge to man as lover and artist: how is such raw grief to be accepted and transformed by the poet into a thing of beauty? Even Orpheus the musician fails, through lack of discipline, to rescue his beloved from death. Each of the three tragic changes in this series of pictures is witnessed intensely and at close range by the lover; Venus is last seen with her mouth on the mouth of Adonis' corpse (ll. 189-92):

> Boca con boca, coge la postrera
> parte del aire que solía dar vida
> al cuerpo por quien ella en este suelo
> aborrecido tuvo al alto cielo.

These three sequences of mythological scenes are presented as close parallels; the only gradation is perhaps one of slight crescendo. The fourth nymph's tapestry forms of course another parallel, but here certain differences are emphasized. Nise has deliberately abandoned ancient mythology; she depicts the Tagus itself (which thus, as Spitzer, *59,* has pointed out, figures on both planes within our poem), the city of Toledo, and the irrigated valley. Then, in this contemporary Spanish setting, woodland goddesses are seen to weep for a dead nymph, whose presence is evoked in the poem's most poignant lines, occurring precisely in the fifth, or middle, stanza of this series of nine (ll. 229-32):

> Cerca del agua, en un lugar florido,
> estaba entre las hierbas degollada
> cual queda el blanco cisne cuando pierde
> la dulce vida entre la hierba verde.

(Here again, for full stylistic analysis, we must turn to Dámaso Alonso.) On a tree one of the goddesses carves an epitaph, and in it Nemoroso is mentioned for the first time. But the lover himself never actually appears; like the hidden face of Timanthes' Agamemnon, Nemoroso's grief cannot be directly depicted, since it exceeds the limits of art just as it exceeds the depicted grief of Orpheus, Apollo and Venus. For Nemoroso's own expression of his grief, we are referred, in lines 250-2, to the First Eclogue; Nise simply wishes to spread throughout the kingdom of Neptune, down along the Tagus to Portugal, the sad story already published among the shepherds of Castile.

This indirect presentation of Nemoroso, who in some way certainly represents Garcilaso himself, is an elaborate example of emphasis by classical understatement. We recall Nemoroso's lament for the dead Elisa in the First Eclogue. The fertile landscape which had been the setting for their happiness together ("Corrientes aguas, puras, cristalinas...") was then like a desert, overrun with sterile thistles, the witnesses of his cruel grief; his only hope was in a new life, with her, after death. But now, in the Third Eclogue, Nemoroso's grief is hidden behind many veils. It is the echo of his voice that we hear, as the single word "Elisa" resounds from mountain to river; this echo occurs in the epitaph which the dead Elisa is represented as speaking by the woodland goddess who carves it upon a tree. And the goddess herself is but a secondary figure within the woven scene which depicts primarily the dead nymph.

In each of the three mythological sequences the lament of the bereft lover, directly represented, was the climax dominating the final lines of the sequence. Nise, deliberately rejecting "de los pasados casos la memoria", presents a sequence which is geographically and chronologically more immediate to poet and reader alike; yet this more recent Spanish story paradoxically recedes into the past as it becomes the fourth tapestry hung in a gallery of ancient *exempla*. [24] And, as has been shown, Nemoroso's grief likewise recedes into the distance, becoming a quotation within a picture ... If in the First Eclogue Nemoroso was Garcilaso's full-scale self-portrait, in the Third Eclogue the artist almost completely effaces himself as a *persona* and yet carefully permits us to catch a glimpse of him as though projected upon the distantly glimmering plane of Velázquez's mirror. [25] Nemoroso's grief-stricken face is now heavily veiled; but, reading closely, we are constantly aware of the presence of Garcilaso, the increasingly self-conscious artist, capable of competing with the poets of classical antiquity.

With the concluding stanza of the central section we are brought back, explicitly, to the question of "artificio", of

[24] The concrete *exemplum* (case or example) was used rhetorically to illustrate an abstract principle. It was traditional to refer to well-known stories; here Garcilaso deliberately adds a new one to the series.

[25] In Velázquez's painting of *Las Meninas,* we see the artist himself in the left foreground, and in the background a distant reflection of the king and queen, presumably standing near the viewer as they visit the studio. Complex perspectives of this sort had been developed, as we now understand, in literary texts such as Garcilaso's Third Eclogue and Cervantes's *Don Quixote*.

artistry. Spitzer (59) has explained fully the ancient and Renaissance theories of chiaroscuro implicit in this stanza; Garcilaso may well have had in mind some phrase such as that of León Battista Alberti: "Light and shade make things appear to stand in relief". [26] He was also certainly aware of a long literary tradition, beginning with Homer, which provides many antecedents not only for the description (ekphrasis) in a poem of artistically depicted scenes, whether forged, carved, painted, or woven, but also for simultaneous commentary, of a more or less technical sort, upon the wonders of artistic illusion. Whatever passages from classical authors Garcilaso may have had in the back of his mind, he himself concentrated in this instance upon the illusion of a third dimension created upon a flat surface by shading. He knew that background "sombras" and foreground "cuerpos" or highlights are in actuality both equally "vain" in the sense of "unreal"; and yet the depicted objects suggest by their appearance that one could grasp them. The fact that Renaissance art can compete in this way with nature itself poses once more the question of art's relation to nature. It is technical skill, the new artifice of perspective, which allows the artist to produce a natural-looking painting and even to improve upon the natural scene being imitated. Similarly it is Garcilaso's art which allows him to use the pastoral conventions in so apparently natural a way that we are convinced of his sincerity; his poetry can thus compete with non-artistic human experiences of love and death and can claim a profounder and more lasting mode of existence.

The foregoing formalistic considerations are part of the poetic substance of the Third Eclogue. Even so natural a force as the Tagus functions in part with the aid of human ingenuity, for it is made to drive its own irrigation wheels, in stanza 27. The reader cannot ignore the poet's concern with the relationship between appearance and reality, art and nature, for he is constantly being reminded that none of the scenes is represented as actually taking place; myths are woven

[26] "Il lume e l'ombra fanno parere le cose rilevate" (*Della pittura*, 1436).

into fabrics which are themselves verbal fictions. But neither can the reader ignore the constant theme of these myths, a complex human experience of love, death, and grief. It is the cruel power of love which inspired Orpheus and which made him look back and lose Eurydice a second time; which brought the goddess Venus down from Olympus and prostrated her upon the bleeding corpse of Adonis. In contrast to the immediate physical violence of these ancient myths, the almost contemporary death of Elisa is tempered by a distantly elegiac tone. Only one word, "degollada", whose unexpected brutality has provoked discussion among commentators, betrays the underlying violence even here; the colors are not exclusively white and green, for into the grass trickles red blood, abstractly metaphorized as "la dulce vida" itself. The last four lines of stanza 29 are the very heart of the poem, and in them we see the outrageous death of a beautiful young woman redeemed by imagery drawn from a realm of swans where death seems natural and even, pictorially and musically, beautiful. For the swan becomes a poet who sings as he dies; "la dulce vida" is not a mere stream of blood trickling through the grass, but like the stream in the *locus amoenus* of stanza 8, it flows musically. In the figure of the swan, Elisa and the poet are joined, and death gives rise to song.

The final thirteen stanzas begin with sunset, fish jumping on the river, and the sound of approaching shepherds singing antiphonally. We have left the static pictorial world for a more immediate plane of temporal reality, in which there is motion and music. Although their songs are poems within a poem, this is not so much a serious new world of artistic illusion as a game whereby the shepherds are amusing themselves. It is a singing contest; the theme is one of love fulfilled in a pastoral setting. The shepherds are rejoining their ladies at nightfall; their reunion, like the return of spring, renews the fertility of the fields themselves. Flérida and Phyllis seem to surpass even the gods, to incarnate the vital forces of nature. There is no shadow of death anywhere. Upon returning to the *locus amoenus* of nymphs and shepherds, which we have seen as belonging to the primary Ovidian world, the reader abandons all tragedies of the past; life in the present is natural, simple, and happy again. Yet this too, one realizes, is a world of illusion, as the nymphs slip away into the waves (ll. 375-6):

> ... y de la blanca espuma que movieron
> las cristalinas ondas se cubrieron.

The dream is over.

It is not, in conclusion, a simple matter to deduce from the Third Eclogue as a whole some clearcut message concerning love and death, nature and art. This poem obviously represents a step beyond the First Eclogue in sophistication: whereas the laments of Salicio and Nemoroso were presented directly and with no more irony than that implicit in the pastoral convention, in the Third Eclogue the complex problem of artistic imitation or representation becomes itself a poetic theme. For art, besides imitating nature, does imitate art, that is, work with and renovate certain traditional conventions. Not since the publication of El Brocense's notes to Garcilaso's poetry in 1574 has anyone been able seriously to pretend that Garcilaso was a simple soul responding with romantic immediacy to a purely amatory experience; the courtly and classical allusions, the "artificios" and "ingenium" underlying almost every line of his eclogues indicate that for him both universal human situations and ancient poetry, both nature and art, entered into what we may call his primary experience of life and into his intuitive or elaborative process. In the Third Eclogue Garcilaso is most fully aware of the implications of this Renaissance view of poetic art.

Within a pastoral framework of nymphs and shepherds are set the varying temporal and spatial perspectives of the embroidered fabrics. By comparison with these central scenes the framework seems quite simple; yet even the pastoral convention, as we have seen, depends upon a non-shepherdly, an artificial, point of view. For the humanist like Garcilaso, art neither exists entirely apart from nature, nor is it simply an object reducible to nature. Man has, for example, artificially made waterwheels part of the natural landscape; in fact the landscape, as a landscape, does not exist until seen by the eye of man, the potential painter. And the pictorial artist uses natural materials, which have been artificially prepared, to express a vision of nature. As a mere object the picture is still part of the natural world; but with the three-dimensional illusion which it presents to the human eye, the artistic object reminds man of his own radically ambiguous mode of existence. Thus, in the Third Eclogue, it is art which orders and simplifies nature, rendering it intelligible; it is a clear sense of artistic distance which converts grief into beauty. As this humanistic dream attains perfect verbal expression, Garcilaso's poetic achievement is complete.

7. *Conclusion*

W HEREAS the prose fiction and the theater of the Spanish Golden Age had a considerable effect upon the subsequent development of European literature, Spanish poetry has been more influenced than influential. Some of Spain's folk poetry, its songs and ballads, was successfully exported under Romantic auspices. But its learned poetry, important within the history of Spanish literature, has seldom crossed international frontiers. (A special case is Portugal, a literary province of Spain during most of the sixteenth and seventeenth centuries.) In the Middle Ages it was the poetry of France and Provence that dominated the scene, in Spain as in the rest of Europe; medieval epic, religious and courtly poetry followed the route of the pilgrims from the French frontier toward Santiago, or St James, of Compostella. Later Italy's *dolce stil nuovo,* Dantesque and Petrarchan, began to infiltrate the Iberian conquerors of Sicily and Naples.

The influence of Italian humanism grew steadily in Spain during the fifteenth century. Toward the middle of that century the Marquis of Santillana wrote a whole series of sonnets in Spanish. Thus Spanish was the first language to assimilate the genre which was most typical of Italian Renaissance poetry. But Santillana's rather clumsy sonnets were not published. And it was not until 1526 that Juan Boscán, in Granada, was encouraged to experiment once more with the Italian hendecasyllable, or iambic pentameter. Boscán, a Catalan-speaker from Barcelona, was a master of Castilian prose, as proven by his translation of Castiglione's *Cortigiano.* But his Castilian poetry too is rather prosaic; it is at its best in the Horatian epistle that he wrote to Mendoza. Boscán never achieved the melodious lyric tone that his younger friend Garcilaso finally developed.

Garcilaso had deep family roots in the provincial life and the conservative traditions of Toledo, the capital of New Castile. But, unlike his older brother, he joined at an early age the court of the new Hapsburg king and supported the monarchy against local feudal rebels. The atmosphere of Charles V's court was Erasmian and international. Garcilaso travelled to Italy, France and Germany before settling in Naples as an important member of the Spanish Viceroy's cosmopolitan court. As courtier, courier and warrior, his experiences encouraged the development of a European, rather than a merely Toledan, point of view.

Garcilaso's development as a poet parallels his political and military career. He began by writing short octosyllabic poems in the tradition of the fifteenth-century Spanish *cancioneros*; witty abstractions and word-play were used to express the exquisite tortures of masochistic love in the troubadour mode. Under the guidance of Boscán, Garcilaso was led to discover the deeper passion and metaphors of the Valencian poet Ausias March; these, combined with the sonnet form and humanistic culture of Petrarch, began to enrich Garcilaso's style, freeing it from the narrow limits of the medieval Spanish tradition of courtly love. Many of his sonnets and most of his *canciones* illustrate what we may call his intermediate style, most typically characterized by a harsh allegorical or psychological road leading over steep mountains toward a distant "belle dame sans merci".

But many of Garcilaso's sonnets are quite different. We can assume that these date from after his arrival in Naples. Mythological and plastic elements reflect the influences of Sannazaro and Ariosto, of Virgil, Horace, Ovid and the elegiac poets. Daphne is transformed into a tree, and Apollo weeps; nymphs in crystalline submarine palaces listen to Garcilaso's sad sweet tears. We catch glimpses of a pastoral landscape in Canción III.

Garcilaso's mature style reaches full development with the discovery and adaptation of several classical genres: the

Horatian ode, the epistle, the elegy, the eclogue. In the first three of these the poet addresses an individual friend discursively; the themes of love, friendship and death are treated in a conversational way, somewhat in the mode of a Montaignean essay. In the eclogues, on the other hand, the poet, if present at all, speaks primarily as poet; but the principal characters assume the fictional masks of shepherds and nymphs. In this pastoral world we rediscover the beauty of nature and of "natural" man; in this world even suffering and grief are aesthetically beautiful.

Garcilaso established the basic idiom of Spanish poetry for centuries to come. It is safe to say that no poet since 1550 has written in the Spanish language without being influenced, directly or indirectly, by his poetry. Fray Luis de León's poetry is very close to Garcilaso's. And even Góngora's baroque poetry can be viewed in large part as a highly original elaboration of Garcilaso's classicism. Some of Quevedo's poetry marks more of a break with this tradition. Neo-classical poetry of the eighteenth century returned to a direct imitation of Garcilaso and Fray Luis, and the Spanish and Spanish-American Romantics retained a great deal of this classical poetic diction. Modern symbolist and post-symbolist poetry in Spanish, beginning with Rubén Darío toward the end of the nineteenth century, continues frequently to echo the sweet nostalgic cadences of Garcilaso. Garcilaso did for the Spanish language what Dante and Petrarch had done for Italian: he invented, or discovered, its classical poetic style. He cultivated and expressed his own feelings by means of ideas, phrases and images which he borrowed from the Greek and Latin tradition and grafted upon the Spanish language. Source-hunting has obscured the originality of this process, which like the most elementary human activities is simultaneously imitative and creative. Using Georges Cirot's metaphor *(28)*, we may say that he designed and executed new mosaics while searching the ruins of ancient temples for appropriate fragments. The creative process is a complex one; the results in Garcilaso's case constitute an essential part of the Spanish language and its poetic tradition.

Appendix: Texts

DURING his brief career as courtier and soldier, Garcilaso published no poetry. We cannot date his earlier poems with any precision, but we have reason to take his Canción III and his 1532 confinement to the island in the Danube as marking a major turning point. He must already by then have written his few short octosyllabic poems. His Canciones I, II and IV, with certain of his sonnets, also written by 1532, reflect his assimilation of the new Italian metrics; in many respects their style is still close to the witty abstractions of the fifteenth-century Spanish *cancioneros,* but we can see the increasingly strong influences of the Italian Petrarch and the Valencian Ausias March. It is between 1532 and his death in 1536 that Garcilaso wrote all of his classical works: an Horatian ode, two elegies, an Horatian epistle, and three eclogues, as well as most of his best sonnets. (By "Horatian" I mean in imitation of the Latin poet Horace.) It was in his Neapolitan period too that he wrote his three surviving Latin poems.

Garcilaso's major Spanish poems are dedicated to a lady in Naples, to his fellow-poet Boscán in Barcelona, and to three members of the Toledo family: to Don Pedro the Viceroy, to his wife and to his nephew, the Duke of Alva. We may assume that he sent final revised copies to these people, except perhaps in the case of the Third Eclogue, written close to the end of his life and apparently never revised or copied perfectly. This was probably the only circulation that Garcilaso was concerned with. We know of only one surviving manuscript that is independent of the printed tradition, for which Boscán was responsible.

After his friend's death in 1536, Boscán took pains to perfect his collection of Garcilaso manuscripts, some of which were certainly written in the poet's own hand. According to the prologue which Boscán's widow wrote, "en el cuarto [libro] quería poner las obras de Garcilaso de la Vega, de las cuales se encargó Boscán por el amistad grande que entrambos mucho tiempo tuvieron, y porque, después de la muerte de Garcilaso, le entregaron a él sus obras para que las dejase como debían de estar". Thus it is to Boscán that we owe the survival and publication of Garcilaso's poetry.

It was more than five years after Garcilaso's death, in March 1542, that Boscán signed a formal contract with a bookseller for the publication of a volume entitled *Las obras de Boscan y algunas de Garcilasso de la Vega repartidas en quatro libros*. A thousand copies were to be well printed on good paper. But while it was being printed, a gathering at a time, Boscán had to leave Barcelona on a trip with the Duke of Alva, and he died while away, in September 1542. The following year his widow had the printing completed, with copyrights for ten years granted by Charles V and by the king of Portugal. Despite these copyrights, pirated reprints appeared almost immediately, both in Barcelona and in Lisbon; but Boscán's widow seems to have been able to have them suppressed. In 1544 two more reprints appeared, one in Spain and one in the Low Countries, and during the following thirteen years the Boscán edition was reprinted at least once a year. This was clearly a best-seller of the mid-sixteenth century. The poetry of Boscán and Garcilaso circulated widely and established definitively the new Italian style in Spanish poetry. A conservative nationalistic reaction had negligible consequences.

In the introduction to his Book II, which was his Petrarchan *canzoniere* of ninety sonnets and ten *canciones,* Boscán speaks with scorn of Spanish *coplas* and with praise of the new style, "more serious and more artistic and, if I am not mistaken, far superior". He then explains how, in Granada in 1526, Navagero had urged him to try the new style in Spanish, and how Garcilaso had encouraged him by precept

and by example. Boscán's three books of somewhat harsh
verse served as an introduction to the final book containing
his friend's much briefer selection, of a more refined aesthetic
quality: a *canzoniere* of twenty-nine sonnets and four *canciones,* one ode, two elegies and one epistle, three eclogues. The
eclogues, in particular, were a new experience for the Spanish
reader, unlike anything in Boscán: a sensuous pastoral world
of ideal landscapes and of sweet sorrow for love lost. Garcilaso's superiority was immediately recognized.

At last in 1569 an enterprising book-seller of Salamanca
published the first independent edition of Garcilaso's poetry,
omitting the works of Boscán. This edition is dedicated to the
rector of the University of Salamanca, and in it we find evidence that the publisher had accepted emendations suggested
by some of the university professors. A Madrid reprint appeared in 1570. And a great humanist of Salamanca, Francisco Sánchez de las Brozas, known as el Brocense, elected to
the Professorship of Rhetoric in 1573, continued to study
intensively the works of Garcilaso, until in 1574 he published
the scholarly edition which would become standard for the
end of the sixteenth and beginning of the seventeenth centuries.
He not only emended the text with care and good judgment;
he also found a few short unpublished poems (sonnets and
coplas), and annotated many classical and Italian sources. This
edition was republished, with a few revisions, in 1577, 1581,
1589, 1600, 1604 and 1612. With this Brocense edition, Garcilaso was canonized as the classical poet of Spain.

That canonization was confirmed by a scholarly poet of
Seville, Fernando de Herrera, who in 1580 published another
edition of Garcilaso, also carefully emended, with much more
voluminous annotations. More than just an edition of Garcilaso, this was an encyclopedia of poetic erudition, a course in
Renaissance theory of poetry. The notes are interspersed with
brief *discursos* or treatises on various subjects which Herrera
considered important for the more erudite poet and reader.
Because he occasionally criticized Garcilaso's own usage, and
because of regional rivalries, Herrera was attacked anonymously by a friend of Francisco Sánchez de las Brozas, and

there ensued a deplorably violent controversy of little real consequence so far as Garcilaso's poetry itself is concerned.

A final scholarly edition was published in 1622 by Tomás Tamayo de Vargas, of Toledo. His text closely resembles that of el Brocense, but he occasionally prefers Herrera's readings. His notes too resemble el Brocense's, although they owe something to the Herrera controversy. With this edition of 1622 the popularity of Garcilaso's poetry seems to begin declining in the face of a new, more sophisticated poetry, that of Góngora and Quevedo. Of the great poets of the seventeenth century, only Lope de Vega maintained occasionally a stylistic level similar to that of Garcilaso.

In the second half of the sixteenth century, Garcilaso's influence had been everywhere apparent. The pastoral romance created in the 1550s by the Portuguese Jorge de Montemayor, *La Diana,* is filled with echoes of Garcilaso's eclogues. The Augustinian Professor of Scripture at Salamanca, and el Brocense's friend, Luis de León, drew directly upon the poetry of Virgil and Horace; but his Spanish style, in his pastoral and Horatian odes, is clearly dependent upon that of Garcilaso, even though in attitude he is less pagan, more explicitly Christian. Garcilaso's poetry was also the point of departure for the rich flowering of sensuous poetry in Andalusia, especially in Herrera's Seville. And at the same time, in Granada, we observe the strange phenomenon of a religious parody, or line-for-line Christianization, of the poetry of Boscán and Garcilaso, published by Sebastián de Córdoba in 1575. This religious poetry, although not always of high quality itself, had a direct influence upon Spain's greatest mystic poet, St John of the Cross, who merges the pastoral world of Garcilaso with that of the Song of Solomon. For the more ascetic Spanish authors, pastoral and chivalric literature were equally sinful and dangerous from a moral point of view. Cervantes, with his own pastoral romance (*La Galatea,* 1585), was obviously steeped in the letter and the spirit of Garcilaso; but he developed an overtly ironic attitude toward pastoral and chivalric myths by the time he published his masterpieces, *Don Quijote* and the *Novelas ejemplares,* in the early seventeenth century.

In the seventeenth century everyone continued to pay lip-service to Garcilaso, whose reputation was still high among classical scholars. In the controversies which raged concerning Góngora's literary heresy, known satirically as *culteranismo,* Garcilaso's authority was frequently cited, both pro and con. Góngora, and Quevedo as well, were in fact elaborators of the poetic tradition established by Garcilaso. But the latter's classical balance and sweetness were inevitably distorted beyond recognition by the elaborations, the ironic sophistication and toughness of the baroque masters. After the Tamayo de Vargas edition of Garcilaso (1622) there was a long gap before a new annotated edition was done by Nicolás de Azara in 1765. Azara's edition, with brief notes drawn from the older commentators, was often reprinted in the eighteenth and nineteenth centuries; it stands at the threshold of a growing new appreciation of Garcilaso's poetry.

Bibliographical Note

Abbreviations of frequently cited journals:

BH: *Bulletin Hispanique*
HR: *Hispanic Review*
MLN: *Modern Language Notes*
MLR: *Modern Language Review*

A. PRINCIPAL EDITIONS OF GARCILASO'S POETRY

1. *Las obras de Boscán y algunas de Garcilasso de la Vega, repartidas en quatro libros,* Barcelona, 1543.
2. *Obras del excelente poeta Garcilasso de la Vega, con anotaciones y enmiendas del licenciado Francisco Sánchez, cathedratico de rhetórica,* Salamanca, 1574; 1577; 1581; 1589; Madrid, 1600; Salamanca, 1604; Madrid, 1612; Geneva, 1765.
3. *Obras de Garcilasso de la Vega con anotaciones de Fernando de Herrera,* Sevilla, 1580; pretends to ignore the preceding edition.
4. *Garcilasso de la Vega, natural de Toledo, príncipe de los poetas castellanos, de don Thomás Tamaio de Vargas,* Madrid, 1622; takes into account editions *2* and *3,* as well as the controversy provoked by *3.*
5. *Obras de Garcilaso de la Vega, ilustradas con notas* de A. de Azara, Madrid, 1765; 1786; 1788; 1796; Barcelona, 1804; Madrid, 1817; 1821; 1860. Azara's brief notes draw upon editions *2, 3* and *4.*
6. *Garcilaso, Obras,* ed. Tomás Navarro Tomás, Madrid: Espasa-Calpe, 1911; 1924; 1935; 1948, etc. Based on Herrera's text; useful introduction, uneven notes.
7. *Garcilasso de la Vega, Works: A Critical Text with a Bibliography,* ed. Hayward Keniston, New York: Hispanic Society, 1925. Based on the first edition, with an excellent bibliography of early editions and a selection of notes. Reviewed by Rüffler (*56*).
8. *Garcilaso de la Vega, Poésies,* ed. & trans. Paul Verdevoye, Paris: Aubier, 1947. Spanish text based on first edition; useful introduction, translation and brief notes.
9. *Garcilaso de la Vega, Obras completas,* ed. Elias L. Rivers, Madrid: Castalia; Columbus: Ohio State University Press, 1964; 1968. Plain text based on the first edition.

10. *Garcilaso de la Vega y sus comentaristas,* ed. Antonio Gallego Morell, Granada: Universidad, 1966; Madrid: Gredos, 1972. Text based on Herrera's; reprints annotations from editions 2 (1574), *3, 4* and *5.*

11. Garcilaso de la Vega, *Poesías castellanas completas,* ed. Elias L. Rivers, Madrid: Castalia, 1960. A modernized text with minimal notes.

12. *Garcilaso de la Vega, Obras completas con comentario,* ed. Elias L. Rivers, Madrid: Castalia; Columbus: Ohio State University Press, 1974. A critical edition with extensive commentaries from scholars of various periods.

B. STUDIES

Books

13. Keniston, Hayward, *Garcilaso de la Vega: A Critical Study of his Life and Works,* New York: Hispanic Society, 1922. A near-definitive biography and a scholarly study of the poems and their sources.

14. Arce Blanco, Margot, *Garcilaso de la Vega: contribución al estudio de la lírica española del siglo XVI (Revista de Filología Española,* anejo XIII), Madrid: Centro de Estudios Históricos, 1930; Río Piedras: Universidad de Puerto Rico, 1961. Studies Garcilaso's themes and ideas as typical of the Renaissance.

15. Lapesa, Rafael, *La trayectoria poética de Garcilaso,* Madrid: Revista de Occidente, 1948; 1968. Studies the development of Garcilaso's art from the Spanish tradition through Ausias March and Petrarch to Sannazaro's classicism.

16. Rivers, Elias L., ed., *La poesía de Garcilaso: ensayos críticos,* Barcelona: Ariel, 1974. A collection of modern studies, from Azorín to Alberto Blecua.

17. Gicovate, Bernard, *Garcilaso de la Vega* (Twayne's World Authors Series, 349), Boston: Twayne, 1975. A general introduction for English-reading non-specialists.

18. Ghertman, Sharon, *Petrarch and Garcilaso: A Linguistic Approach to Style,* London: Tamesis, 1975. Applies the method of Riffaterre.

19. Prieto, Antonio, *Garcilaso de la Vega,* Madrid: S. G. E. L., 1975. A lively narrative life-and-works.

Articles

20. Alatorre, Antonio, "Garcilaso, Herrera, Prete Jacopín y Don Tomás Tamayo de Vargas", *MLN,* LXXVIII (1963), 126-51. Revised version in *16,* pp. 323-65. Tamayo's use of Prete Jacopín's critique of Herrera.

21. Alatorre, Antonio, "Sobre la 'gran fortuna' de un soneto de Garcilaso", *Nueva Revista de Filología Hispánica,* XXIV (1975), 142-77. A study of the classical origins and Golden Age imitations of Sonnet XXIX.

22. Alonso, Dámaso, *Poesía española: ensayo de métodos y límites estilísticos* (Madrid: Gredos, 1950), pp. 49-108. A stylistic analysis of a few stanzas from the Third Eclogue.

23. Arce Blanco, Margot, "La Égloga segunda de Garcilaso", *Asomante,* V (1949), no. 1, 57-73; no. 2, 60-78. An analysis of form and content.

24. Arce Blanco, Margot, "La Égloga primera de Garcilaso", *La Torre,* L, 2 (1953), 31-68. An analysis of form and content.

25. Arce Blanco, Margot, "Cerca el Danubio una isla...", in *Studia philologica: homenaje ofrecido a Dámaso Alonso,* I (Madrid: Gredos, 1960), pp. 91-100. Reprinted in *16,* pp. 103-17. An analysis of form and content.

26. Azar, Inés, "La textualidad de la *Égloga II* de Garcilaso", *MLN,* XCIII (1978), 176-208.

27. Bohigas, Pere, "Más sobre la Canción IV de Garcilaso", *Ibérida,* 5 (June, 1961), 79-90. The influence of Ausias March.

28. Cirot, Georges, "A propos des dernières publications sur Garcilaso de la Vega", *BH,* XXII (1920), 234-55. A useful analysis of Navarro Tomás *(6)* and others, with suggestions for improvement.

29. Consiglio, Carlo, "I sonetti di Garcilaso de la Vega: problemi critici", *Annali del Corso di Lingue e Letterature Straniere, Università di Bari,* II (1954), 215-74. An overly ambitious attempt to date each sonnet precisely.

30. Dunn, Peter N., "Garcilaso's Ode *A la Flor de Gnido:* A Commentary on Some Renaissance Themes and Ideas", *Zeitschrift für romanische Philologie,* LXXXI (1965), 288-309. Spanish trans. in *16,* pp. 127-62. The Horatian sources, "Gnido", Venus, imitation and virtuosity.

31. Fernández-Morera, Darío, "Garcilaso's Second Eclogue and the Literary Tradition", *HR,* XLVII (1979), 37-53.

32. Gallego Morell, Antonio, "La escuela de Garcilaso", *Arbor,* XVII (1950), 27-47. Defines the first group of Italianate poets in Spain.

33. García Rey, Verardo, "Nuevas noticias referentes al poeta Garcilaso de la Vega", *Boletín de la Sociedad Española de Excursiones,* XXXIV (1926), 287-302 and XXXV (1927), 71-91. Bibliographical data.

34. Glaser, Edward, "Garcilaso's Minnesklave", *MLN,* LXX (1955), 198-203. The iconography of Venus, and its tradition.

35. Goodwyn, Frank, "Garcilaso de la Vega, Representative in the Spanish Cortes", *MLN,* LXXXII (1967), 225-9. Biographical data.

36. Goodwyn, Frank, "New Light on the Historical Setting of Garcilaso's Poetry", *HR,* XLVI (1978), 1-22. More biographical data; argues against significance of Isabel Freire (see *61*).

37. Green, Otis H., in his *Spain and the Western Tradition: The Castilian Mind in Literature from El Cid to Calderón*, I (Madison: University of Wisconsin Press, 1963), pp. 138-60. Analyzes Garcilaso's courtly and Platonic ideas concerning love.

38. Guillén, Claudio, "Sátira y poética en Garcilaso", in *Homenaje a Casalduero* (Madrid: Gredos, 1972), pp. 209-33. An important study of genre: elegy, satire, epistle.

39. Iventosch, Herman, "Garcilaso's Sonnet 'Oh dulces prendas': A Composite of Classical and Medieval Models", *Annali dell' Istituto Universitario Orientale di Napoli, Sezione Romanza*, VII (1965), 203-27. A thorough study.

40. Jones, Royston O., "Garcilaso, poeta del humanismo", *Clavileño*, 28 (July-August 1954), 1-7. Reprinted in *16*, pp. 51-70. Garcilaso as a philosophical poet in whom reason and art come to control passion and grief.

41. Jones, Royston O., "The Idea of Love in Garcilaso's Second Eclogue", *MLR*, XLVI (1951), 388-95. Second Eclogue as a development of Canción IV, urging the control of lust by reason and heroic discipline.

42. Lapesa, Rafael, "El cultismo semántico en la poesía de Garcilaso", *Revista de Estudios Hispánicos* (Puerto Rico), II (1972), 33-45. Reprinted in his *Poetas y prosistas de ayer y de hoy* (Madrid: Gredos, 1977), pp. 92-109. A study of subtle Latinisms.

43. Lida [de Malkiel], María, "Transmisión y recreación de temas grecolatinos en la poesía lírica española", *Revista de Filología Hispánica*, I (1939), 20-63; revised version in her *La tradición clásica en España* (Barcelona: Ariel, 1975), 35-117. The nightingale, the wounded stag and Flérida.

44. Lumsden, Audrey, "Problems Connected with the Second Eclogue of Garcilaso de la Vega", *HR*, XV (1947), 251-71. Poem's parts united by Severo; psychological intensity (madness) as primary poetic value.

45. Lumsden, Audrey, "Garcilaso and the Chatelainship of Reggio", *MLR*, XLVII (1952), 559-60. Documents reconciliation of the poet with Charles V.

46. Macdonald, Inez, "La segunda égloga de Garcilaso", *Boletín del Instituto Español* (London), 12 (Oct. 1950), 6-11. Reprinted in *16*, pp. 209-35. Poem analyzed as a debate between Albanio's sensual madness and the Duke's heroic sanity, with due attention given to symbols of water, wind and hunt.

47. Mele, Emilio, "Las poesías latinas de Garcilaso de la Vega y su permanencia en Italia", *BH*, XXV (1923), 108-48 and 361-70; XXVI (1924), 35-51. A general study of the Neapolitan background.

48. Mele, Emilio, "In margine alle poesie de Garcilaso", *BH*, XXXII (1930), 218-45. Notes concerning classical and Italian sources.

49. Parker, Alexander A., "Theme and Imagery in Garcilaso's First Eclogue", *Bulletin of Spanish Studies*, XXV (1948), 222-7. Spanish trans. in *16*, pp. 197-208. An analysis of the philosophical and poetic unity of the work.

50. Paterson, Alan K. G., "Ecphrasis in Garcilaso's *Égloga tercera*", *MLR*, LXXII (1977), 73-92. Poetry as the description of pictorial art.

51. Rendall, Stephen F., and Miriam D. Sugarmon, "Imitation, Theme and Structure in Garcilaso's First Elegy", *MLN*, LXXXII (1967), 230-7. A thorough analysis and defense of the poem's unity.

52. Rivers, Elias L., "The Horatian Epistle and its Introduction into Spanish Literature", *HR*, XXII (1954), 175-94. Concentrates on Garcilaso's epistle.

53. Rivers, Elias, "The Pastoral Paradox of Natural Art", *MLN*, LXXVII (1962), 130-44. Spanish trans. in *16*, pp. 285-308. An analysis of the relationship between nature and art in the Third Eclogue.

54. Rivers, Elias L., "Albanio as Narcissus in Garcilaso's Second Eclogue", *HR*, XLI (1973), 297-304. On the allegorical use of myth.

55. Roig, Adrien, "¿Quiénes fueron Salicio y Nemoroso?", *Criticón*, IV (1978), 1-36. Argues cogently that Salicio represents the Portuguese poet Sá de Miranda, also an admirer of Isabel Freire.

56. Rüffler, Adolf, "Zur Garcilaso-Frage", *Archiv für das Studium der neueren Sprachen und Literaturen*, CLIII (1928), 219-30. A critical review of Keniston's edition *(7)*.

57. Salinas, Pedro, in his *Reality and the Poet in Spanish Poetry* (Baltimore: Johns Hopkins Press, 1940; 1966), 65-93. The "idealization of reality" in Garcilaso.

58. San Román, Francisco B. de, "Garcilaso desterrado de Toledo", *Boletín de la Real Academia de Bellas Artes y Ciencias Históricas de Toledo*, I (1919), 193-9. Biographical data.

59. Spitzer, Leo, "Garcilaso, Third Eclogue, Lines 265-271", *HR*, XX (1952), 243-8. Theories of painting and perspective.

60. Waley, Pamela, "Garcilaso's Second Eclogue Is a Play", *MLR*, LXXII (1977), 585-96. The poem as pastoral court drama.

61. Waley, Pamela, "Garcilaso, Isabel and Elena: the Growth of a Legend", *Bulletin of Hispanic Studies*, LVI (1979) 11-15. Argues that only three poems refer clearly to Isabel Freire and that others may refer to Elena Zúñiga, the poet's wife.

62. Wilson, Edward M., "La estrofa sexta de la canción a la Flor de Gnido", *Revista de Filología Española*, XXXVI (1952), 118-22. Repr. in *16*, pp. 119-26. Defends the text of the first edition.

63. Woods, M. J., "Rhetoric in Garcilaso's First Eclogue", *MLN*, LXXXIV (1969), 143-56. Argues, against Parker *(49)*, that Salicio's song is more rhetorical than philosophical.

Addendum

64. Reisz de Rivarola, Susana, "Transferencias poéticas: Garcilaso de
    la Vega y su 'imitación' de la bucólica virgiliana", *Iberoromania,*
    n.s., 6 (1980 [1977]), 86-121. A close study of intertextuality
    in Eclogue III, lines 297-320.

Renaissance Italy DG 533 LAV.